Censorship on the Internet

From Filters to Freedom of Speech

Wendy Herumin

Enslow Publishers, Inc.

40 Industrial Road   PO Box 38
Box 398   Aldershot
Berkeley Heights, NJ 07922   Hants GU12 6BP
USA   UK

http://www.enslow.com

Library of Congress Cataloging-in-Publication Data

Herumin, Wendy.
  Internet censorship : from filters to freedom of speech / Wendy
Herumin.
    p. cm. — (Issues in focus)
  Includes bibliographical references and index.
  ISBN 0-7660-1946-2 (cloth)
    1. Internet and children—Juvenile literature. 2. Freedom of speech—
Juvenile literature. 3. Internet—Censorship—United States—Juvenile
literature. 4. Internet—Access control—United States—Juvenile litera-
ture. [1. Internet. 2. Freedom of speech.] I. Title. II. Issues in focus
(Hillside, N.J.)
  HQ784.I58H47 2004
    303.48'33—dc21

                                        2003008177

Printed in the United States of America

10 9 8 7 6 5 4 3 2 1

To Our Readers: We have done our best to make sure all Internet
Addresses in this book were active and appropriate when we went to
press. However, the author and the publisher have no control over and
assume no liability for the material available on those Internet sites or on
other Web sites they may link to. Any comments or suggestions can be sent
by e-mail to comments@enslow.com or to the address on the back cover.

Illustration Credits: ArtToday, pp. 13, 23, 79; Corbis Images
Royalty-Free, p. 101; Corel Corporation, pp. 29, 38; reproduced
from the *Dictionary of American Portraits*, published by Dover
Publications, Inc., in 1967, p. 74; ©Engelhardt in the St. Louis
Post-Dispatch/reprinted with permission, p. 68; Eyewire
Images, pp. 48, 61, 89, 92; courtesy of Focus on the Family, p.
17; courtesy of the Freedom Forum, p. 8; courtesy of Kathiann
M. Kowalski, p. 55; Library of Congress, pp. 34, 105; photo by
Drake Mabry, copyright 1965, The Des Moines Register and
Tribune Company, reprinted with permission, p. 65; courtesy of
the Denver Post, p. 83; courtesy of www.fbi.gov, p. 47; courtesy
of Zhou Yan, p. 96.

Cover Illustration: Corel Corporation (background); Hemera
Technologies (monitor); Enslow Publishers, Inc. (inset).

Contents

Acknowledgments

The following people generously shared their time to help the author understand a complex topic: Lorrie Faith Cranor, Researcher, ATT-Labs Research; Steve Watters, Internet Project Manager for Focus on the Family; Judith Krug, Director, Office of Intellectual Freedom for the American Library Association; J. Robert Flores, Administrator, Office of Juvenile Justice and Delinquency Prevention for the U.S. Department of Justice; David Hudson, staff attorney with the First Amendment Center at Vanderbilt University; Nancy Willard, Research Associate, the Responsible Netizen Institute in Eugene, Oregon; Bruce Taylor, President and Chief Counsel for the National Law Center for Children and Families; Deborah Hooker, Principal Consultant, Mnemosyne Consulting; and Aaron Smith, the youngest ever recipient of the "Free Spirit" award.

1

Conflicts in Cyberspace

One afternoon in McKinney, Texas, thirteen-year-old Aaron Smith drew a picture of a rat for a school slide show project. One of his friends thought the rat looked more like a dead Chihuahua.

The boys laughed. Soon they were making up "dead Chihuahua" jokes. By the time class was over, Aaron had an idea for a Web page. He would name it "Chihuahua Haters of the World," or C.H.O.W., and invite visitors to join his online "club."[1]

With the help of his friends, Aaron

developed material for his site. On July 21, 1997, C.H.O.W. was released on the World Wide Web. Aaron and his friends intended the Web page to be fun.

"I have never harmed an animal and I get along great with dogs. The site was only meant to be a joke," said Aaron about his online club.[2]

Most visitors to the Web site understood that C.H.O.W. was a spoof. However, one day an animal lover found the site and became upset. Aaron's Web page was added to a mailing list for activists who defend abused animals.

"My site got fifteen hundred hits in one day. I received over one hundred e-mails from people who were angry. Some were as far away as Montana," said Aaron.[3]

Maybe it was the "mission statement" of C.H.O.W. that upset the animal lovers. The club posted its purpose as follows:

> Here at the C.H.O.W. On-line Embassy and Citadel, we stand for the complete and total annihilation of the chihuahua species. We believe that they are inferior to other dogs; thus [they] must be eliminated and stopped from ever polluting the dog gene pool.[4]

Perhaps the animal lovers took offense at the cartoon page "Uses of a Chihuahua." Under the heading of "transportation," one illustration showed a Chihuahua tied to the bottom of a pair of shoes. Another showed a dog as an "alternate source of energy" when wired to a hair dryer. According to the pictures, Chihuahuas could also be fed to whales, dropped into toilets to solve plumbing problems, or thrown to rats as "rat bait."[5]

Aaron's site mentioned that he had come up with the idea for the club while at school. He stated the name of his middle school but did not provide a link to it. One day Aaron was taken out of English class and sent to the principal's office. Friends who had listed their names on the site were also summoned. Aaron learned that an animal lover had contacted the school and threatened a protest.

The principal told Aaron to write an apology letter to post on the Web. He agreed. But when she ordered him to delete his Web site, Aaron refused. Since he had not created the Web site at school, he did not think that anyone there had the right to tell him to destroy it.[6]

School officials suspended him for the rest of the day and removed him from his Emerging Technologies class. He was told he had violated the school's acceptable use policy. As part of his punishment, he could no longer be an aide in his computer class nor could he access the Internet at school.

Aaron's parents decided to contact the American Civil Liberties Union (ACLU) for help. The ACLU spoke to the school board on Aaron's behalf. The civil liberties organization clarified Aaron's right to free speech under the Constitution. They explained that because he had created the Web site at home, the school did not have the authority to discipline him or to destroy his site. School officials agreed to remove the suspension citation from his school

Aaron Smith was suspended from school for his anti-Chihuahua Web site. But he stood up for his right to free speech.

records. Aaron was also allowed to return to his computer classes.

Later that spring Aaron received the "Free Spirit" award from the Freedom Forum, a nonprofit group devoted to preserving freedom of speech. The honor included a trophy and a free trip to San Francisco for the awards ceremony.[7]

What students can say on off-campus Web sites is one of several issues surrounding online access for minors, people seventeen years old or younger. More controversial still is the information young people find on the Internet. Online pornography concerns many parents, educators, and lawmakers.

Pornography on the Net

According to the National Research Council (NRC), pornography means sexually explicit "material that is used to create sexual arousal or desire."[8] However, the word pornography has no legal definition. People often use the term to mean both *indecency* (a form of sexually explicit material that is protected by the First Amendment) and *obscenity* (a form of sexually explicit material that is not protected).

Pornography is a subjective term. It means different things to different people. You may call a museum exhibit pornographic because the subject matter offends your religious, moral, or aesthetic views, while I consider the display to be art. Because people disagree about what is—or is not— pornographic, the NRC suggests that a better term for unsuitable content for minors is "inappropriate sexually explicit material."[9]

Easy to Find

Children can find sexually explicit material on the Internet. A study of online users in 2000 found that one out of four young people stumbled upon unwanted sexual pictures or other material. Most of the images were found during Internet searches. Unsolicited e-mail, or spam, from unknown sources accounted for the rest.[10]

Students also send pornographic e-mail to each other. Messages typically contain images harvested from *teasers*, says Bruce Taylor of the National Law Center for Children and Families.[11] Teasers are sexually explicit advertisements for commercial adult entertainment sites. The ads urge the viewer to pay a fee (usually with a credit card) to enter the Web site.

One of the main distinctions between online pornography and its counterpart in the physical world is what computer columnist John Dvorak calls "push technology." Dvorak, who describes himself as a free speech advocate, nevertheless complained in a 2002 article about the aggressive tactics used by marketers to promote adult entertainment Web sites. Dvorak wrote:

> I'm sick of it. And I'm not talking about a picture of a pretty girl with no clothes on. Online porn has left simple concepts like that in the dust. The porn purveyors have taken my freedom to choose away from me. Push

technology now pushes porn at me whether I like it or not.[12]

Aside from unsolicited e-mail, marketers may use deceptive links to lead people to porn sites. "Some hard-core operators have hijacked common names, usually anything guys would find interesting such as sports or cars," according to Taylor. "While looking for innocent material, children can find hot links to pornographic sites."[13]

A user who follows a link to a porn site may have trouble getting out. *Mousetrapping* is a popular practice to keep people at a pornographic site. When the user closes one window, another one pops up. Sometimes the only way to get out of a mousetrap is to shut down the computer.

Civil libertarians caution people to put online pornography into context. Although they are easy to find, pornographic images and text account for a small percentage of total Internet content. Out of 2 billion Web pages in 2002, less than 2 percent contained sexually explicit content for adults.[14] And the problem is not specific to the United States. Most commercial pornographers are based in other countries. The NRC estimates that there are four hundred thousand sites worldwide that provide adult entertainment to paying subscribers. Only a fourth of these are in the United States.[15]

Other Net Dangers

Prior to World War II, Adolf Hitler delivered speeches that stirred up public hostility against the Jewish population in Germany. Hitler's vicious language paved the way for the destruction of millions of innocent people. His propaganda was an example of "hate speech."

Hate speech exalts one group of people by denigrating another, often on the basis of race or religion. According to a 2002 report, the Council of Europe took steps to outlaw hate speech on the Internet for its member nations.[16] Many parents and school administrators in the United States also object to having students find sites containing hate speech.

Some parents oppose other types of material, too. These include bomb-making instructions, violence toward animals and humans, profanity, vulgar words, information about illegal drugs, gambling, the sale of alcoholic beverages or tobacco, and sites promoting unlawful business activities, religious cults, radical military groups, or witchcraft.[17]

People More Dangerous Than Images

Potentially harmful strangers pose the greatest threat to children online, said a report from the NRC. Meeting a sexual predator through a chat room or e-mail is far more dangerous than viewing inappropriate images.[18]

A study by the University of New Hampshire found that one in five young people aged ten through seventeen received an unwanted sexual solicitation on the Internet in 2000. Nearly half the young people approached online did not tell anyone about it. However, of those surveyed, less than one

Adolf Hitler spoke against the Jews and other minority groups in Europe, stirring up hatred and violence. Many people see hate speech on the Internet as dangerous.

percent said they had been encouraged by people they met on the Internet to run away from home.[19] After the study's release, President George W. Bush promised to renew law enforcement efforts on the Internet.

In addition to inappropriate content and harmful strangers, a third source of concern for young Internet users is invasion of privacy. In 1998, Congress passed the Children's Online Privacy Protection Act (COPPA), which keeps marketers from buying or selling personal information about children under the age of thirteen. Online safety education programs emphasize the importance of not giving out names and addresses or other personal information over the Internet.

Many people want to protect children from harmful or unpleasant experiences on the Internet. They disagree on what to do.

Protection versus Free Speech

One theory says that education is the answer to protecting children online. Young people should be taught how to safely navigate the Internet and how to think critically about what they find, according to this view. Critical thinking skills include evaluating the source of information, making sound judgments about it, and checking one's conclusions against independent sources, according to Judith Krug, director of the Office for Intellectual Freedom of the American Library Association.[20]

Another approach favors government intervention

in addition to education. This view says that existing obscenity laws should be vigorously enforced. Some in this group say we need new laws, too.

Since 1996, the federal government has passed three laws aimed at protecting minors from inappropriate online content. All three laws sparked debate. All raised First Amendment concerns, and opponents have challenged these laws in court. The Supreme Court struck down the first one, sent back the second one to a lower court, and upheld the third one, known as the Children's Internet Protection Act (CIPA). The CIPA law says that schools and libraries receiving certain federal funds must use technology tools to screen out pornography and materials that are harmful to minors.

Technology tools, such as those mandated by CIPA, are another solution proposed to the problem of keeping children safe. Filtering and blocking systems, or "filters," are software programs that screen out pornographic sites and other types of controversial material. Filters have many supporters who approve of these tools as a way to protect children from accidental or deliberate exposure to inappropriate materials. Opponents point to evidence that filters block substantial amounts of useful and legally protected information. This is known as "over-blocking." Filters also fail to screen out all the potentially offensive material on the Internet, primarily because of the rapid growth of new content.

Parents, teachers, librarians, lawmakers, and members of industry have voiced opinions about how to protect children from harmful experiences without infringing free speech rights for adults. No one has yet offered an answer that satisfies everyone.

The World Joins In

In the United States, some people want to regulate online speech to protect minors. Many other countries share this concern. More repressive governments also object to political dissent, hate speech, and religious blasphemy.

A global survey of the press in 2001 revealed eighteen countries with severely restrictive Internet laws. Those countries included Algeria, China, Cuba, Ethiopia, Kenya, Laos, Russia, and Tunisia. Government officials control Internet service providers in many of these countries. "Citizens are subjected to fines, harassment, imprisonment or worse for dissenting from official policies or for messages deemed seditious," said the survey.[21]

So far, American courts have taken great care to protect free speech rights on the Internet. Legal scholar Robert Corn-Revere says:

> Such a reaction is not unexpected where a free and open medium of communication is compatible with a political system predicated on the free exchange of ideas.[22]

According to Corn-Revere, many other countries see the Internet as a threat. He cites France as an example. In November 2000, a French court ordered Yahoo!, a U.S.-based Internet service provider (ISP), to crack down on sites selling Nazi memorabilia.[23]

Dr. James Dobson, shown here with a group of children, is the founder of Focus on the Family. Like many other conservative Christian groups, it supports filters and other types of parental control on computers.

The French government did not want its citizens to enter such sites, even Web sites based in America. An American court refused to enforce the French court's ruling. As the French case illustrates, the global nature of the Internet raises complex questions for many governments.

2

Exploring
the Internet

Computers that share a common
networking protocol, or language, can
exchange information when linked together
by telecommunication lines or other means.
Computers connected this way form a network. The Internet is a global network
made up of many smaller networks.

The Internet has been growing for
more than three decades. How big is it?
One way to measure size is to count the
number of users online. By September
2002, slightly more than 605 million
people worldwide were using the
Internet.[1]

Researchers and scientists were the first to go online, but today the mainstream public uses the Internet. Many users in the United States are young people. According to a national survey, by 2002, most American children (65 percent) had Internet access at home, at school, or in another location.[2]

A Shared Dream

No single person invented the Internet, but many people and organizations helped it grow. In the late 1960s, an agency at the Department of Defense created the first computer network. The Advanced Research Projects Agency (ARPA) connected four supercomputing centers with high-speed telephone lines so that researchers could exchange data electronically.

The agency named its first network ARPANET. Throughout the 1970s, the defense department added more sites to ARPANET nationwide. Meanwhile, private networks for scientists and researchers also took root.

The National Science Foundation (NSF) took charge of the emerging nationwide network in the 1980s. The agency created a high-speed network called NSFNET that was faster and more powerful than ARPANET and eventually replaced it.

By 1995, companies had begun to advertise and sell products and services on the Internet. The opportunity to conduct business online spurred new growth. More members of the general public began to go online, too. One reason for the Internet's growing popularity was a new service called the World Wide Web.

The World Wide Web

Before 1990, going online was somewhat complicated. If you wanted to download files, send an electronic message, or visit a discussion group, you had to type in commands. Depending on the task, some commands were complex. Users needed a certain amount of training to navigate the Internet successfully.

In the early 1990s, software designer Tim Berners-Lee at the European Particle Physics Lab (CERN) in Switzerland found a simpler way to share information. He used a technology known as *hypertext* to link together documents stored on different computers.

In his book *Weaving the Web*, Berners-Lee explains what he was trying to accomplish. He writes:

> *Suppose all the information stored on computers everywhere were linked,* I thought. *Suppose I could program my computer to create a space in which anything could be linked to anything.* All the bits of information in every computer . . . on the planet . . . would be available to me and to anyone else. There would be a single, global information space.[3]

His "single, global information space" took shape as the World Wide Web. A popular online tutorial explains how the Web works. On a hypertext page, certain words or pictures contain links to other documents. When you select the word or picture, your computer sends a request to the server where the file is stored. The server returns the page you want. You can then view the document on your screen.[4]

Today's Web browsers incorporate colorful graphics, text, and sound. You can listen to music, view animations, or watch a live broadcast of an event. Almost every Internet service—e-mail, file transfers, online discussion groups, and so on—can be accessed through your Web browser. Using these services is rarely more complicated than pointing and clicking with your mouse. Because the Web is lively and easy to use, it is one of the most popular services on the Internet.

Both a Library and a Mall

Supreme Court justice John Paul Stevens describes the World Wide Web as "both a vast library including millions of readily available and indexed publications and a sprawling mall offering goods and services."[5] Universities, the government, and private companies publish information on the World Wide Web. So do nonprofit organizations and individuals.

Like a global library, the Web contains endless resources, ranging from scientific data to news and entertainment. People can search for the menu of a local restaurant or find satellite images of the earth. They can download a video game or learn about the Civil War. Students can listen to the radio, view art, or research in-line skating techniques.

The World Wide Web links users to millions of different sites at the click of a mouse.

The Web is also like a shopping mall with countless products and services for sale. Consumers can purchase anything from chocolates to ski equipment. They can pay bills, make plane reservations, or earn a college degree through "virtual universities."

From the start, the Internet has been a communications tool. Electronic mail links pen pals who live in the same city or in different countries. Newsgroups offer people with similar interests a way to exchange questions and answers. Chat rooms give immediate feedback to participants. In chat rooms, visitors type messages to each other on their computer screens. The messages can be read by anyone participating in the group.

No other form of media—newspapers, radio, or television—offers the average person a comparable opportunity to publish his or her views on such a grand scale.

3

A New Form
of Media

Newspapers, magazines, books, and brochures are popular forms of print media. Publishers use these channels of communication to reach their audiences. The Internet shares some characteristics of the print media. For example, the Internet contains electronic versions of articles, books, and reference materials. Most daily metropolitan newspapers maintain Web sites. Some post breaking news on the Internet.

The Internet also resembles the broadcast media in certain ways. Web users can find video newscasts, radio programs, short animated films and other audio and video products. Live Web broadcasts let viewers see events within seconds of the time they occur.

Although the Internet shares certain characteristics of older forms of media, it has distinctive features. No other form of mass communication provides a global forum for people to meet and share ideas. No other form of media allows the average person to publish to a worldwide audience.

In 1996, Congress passed a law known as the Communications Decency Act (CDA). A court had to decide if the Internet could be regulated for words and images that many people considered "indecent" and "offensive." Civil liberties groups opposed the law. A panel of three federal judges in Philadelphia heard the case.

One of the first things the court had to decide was whether the Internet was like the print media or more like radio and television. Their decision was important, because laws governing the print media are somewhat different from the restrictions placed on over-the-air broadcasts.

Role of the Free Press

The First Amendment in the Bill of Rights defends freedom of speech, religion, and the press. It guarantees citizens the right to speak freely and to meet in public without harassment. It reads:

> Congress shall make no law respecting an establishment of religion, prohibiting the free

exercise thereof; or abridging the freedom of speech, or of the press; or the right of the people peaceably to assemble, and to petition the Government for address of grievances.

In 1971, the Supreme Court upheld the freedom of the press in an important case known as *New York Times Co. v. United States*. Reporters from *The New York Times* and *The Washington Post* had obtained copies of a government study called "History of U.S. Decision-Making Process on Viet Nam Policy."[1] The study was a classified document, meaning that no one other than government officials were supposed to see it. It explained how America had become involved in the Vietnam War.

The government sued the newspapers to keep them from printing the study. They said they wanted to safeguard military and diplomatic secrets. The court disagreed.

Ruling in favor of the newspapers, Justice Hugo Black emphasized the importance of a free press in our democratic society. Our Founding Fathers established the press to serve the people, not to serve government officials, said Black:

> The Government's power to censor the press was abolished so that the press would remain forever free to censure the Government. The press was protected so that it could bare the secrets of government and inform the people.[2]

The two newspapers deserved praise for doing what "the Founders hoped and trusted they would do," said Justice Black.[3]

Broadcast and Print Media

The broadcast media has somewhat different regulations because it is based on a different technology than the printed word. Only a limited number of channels exist for radio and TV stations to use. Stations cannot "own" a frequency, but must ask for the right to use it, because the airwaves are considered public property.

Radio and television are more closely regulated by the government than is the print media. Over-the-air broadcasts reach the public more easily than do printed messages. A person does not need to read or write to understand a television program or a radio newscast. As federal courts have noted, someone must be literate to read a newspaper or a book and must make an effort to find the printed material.

Radio and television broadcasters have to be careful about what they say and when they say it. They do not know who might be listening. They must control programs so that children are protected from language and images intended for adult audiences. The law prohibits over-the-air broadcasters, during certain time periods of the day, from broadcasting words and images that are considered inappropriate for young viewers.

In 1996, the federal district court in Philadelphia ruled that the Internet was more like the print media than the broadcast media. The court overruled the CDA because it violated the principles of free speech. The Supreme Court later upheld this decision.[4]

Those in the broadcasting industry must work to protect children from inappropriate language and images.

The courts have given books, magazines, newspapers, and other print media more freedom from regulation than any other form of mass communication. The Internet now enjoys this high level of freedom. First Amendment attorney and author Robert S. Peck writes:

> The U.S. Supreme Court has concluded that cyberspace receives the highest level of protection that the First Amendment affords. As a result, the same considerations that apply to printed words and images apply as well to the electronic word and the digital image.[5]

Web Censorship in the United States

Nearly ninety countries were online by 1995. You could send an e-mail to President Bill Clinton or visit the Vatican's Web site. You could shop, bank, listen to talk radio, or order pizza on the Web.[1] One half of all school-aged children in the United States had Internet access at school.[2] Mainstream America and the world had embraced a new form of mass communication.

That year also marked a fierce public debate. In June, an engineering student from Carnegie Mellon University (CMU) published a controversial report about online pornography.[3] The study made the cover of *Time* magazine. Many people believed the report was a deliberate attempt to frighten the public. Critics suspected that politicians were influenced erroneously by the information.

Journalists and members of the academic community soundly criticized both the *Time* article and the university study. In fact, the same month that *Time* reported an epidemic of online pornography, a different group of researchers at CMU said ordinary families were not big consumers of sexually explicit materials.[4]

Two professors from Vanderbilt University said that the CMU student misrepresented his case.[5] They pointed out that the student had examined only a specific group of electronic bulletin board systems (BBSs) devoted to pornographic material. Yet he did not present the scope of his study clearly. As a result, readers could get the impression that what was said about the BBSs applied to a larger group of services.[6] The professors found many other problems with the study. They concluded the student probably wanted to give politicians "ammunition" to pass Internet censorship laws.[7]

Senator James Exon of Nebraska did exactly what critics feared. He spoke to Congress about the problem of online pornography.[8] Soon he introduced the Communications Decency Act.

Cleaning Up Cyberspace

In 1996, Congress passed the first major telecommunications bill in thirty-two years. Technology had radically changed since the Telecommunications Act of 1934 that laid down rules for radio, telephone, and telegraphs. Now Congress wanted a new set of regulations.

The Telecommunications Act of 1996 encouraged industry growth. By lifting outdated restrictions, the law made it easier for telephone companies, radio, cable, and broadcast television companies to conduct business.

Before Congress voted on the bill, Senator Exon added the Communications Decency Act as an amendment. Exon said that laws designed to "protect young and old users from harassment and obscenity and indecency" needed to be updated for the Internet.[9] Existing laws already restricted radio and broadcast TV stations from airing certain types of material (such as profanity) during hours of the day when children might be present. Exon wanted speech on the Internet to be equally acceptable for families.

Senator Exon explained his concerns to Congress:

> If in any American neighborhood an individual were distributing pornographic photos, cartoons, videos, and stories to children, or if someone were posting lewd photographs on lampposts and telephone poles for all to see, or if children were welcome to enter and browse adult bookstores and triple X rated video arcades, there would be a public outrage.[10]

That person would probably get arrested, said Senator Exon. He wanted the same type of regulation to govern what he called "America's electronic neighborhood."[11]

The Communications Decency Act

President Clinton signed the telecommunications bill, including the CDA, into law on February 8, 1996. The CDA made it a crime to send indecent or "patently offensive" material over the Internet to a person under the age of eighteen. Offensive material, as defined by the new law, included

> any comment, request, suggestion, proposal, image or other communication that, in context, depicts or describes in terms patently offensive as measured by contemporary community standards, sexual or excretory activities or organs.[12]

For violating the statute, a person could be fined, sent to jail, or both. To avoid prosecution, Web site operators of controversial sites had to make a "good faith" effort to keep minors from finding indecent material. For example, they could establish a credit card verification scheme to screen out minors. (Sites that made visitors use a credit card for admission would presumably be more difficult for minors to enter, since few young people had their own credit cards.)

The act applied to all forms of Internet communication, including e-mail, chat rooms, newsgroups, and the World Wide Web. One analyst complained the CDA was like passing a law to police "phone conversations, faxes, television broadcasts, readings of poetry in coffee houses, private letters, newspaper

President Bill Clinton signed the Telecommunications Act of 1996, which contained the Communications Decency Act (CDA). The CDA prohibited sending indecent material over the Internet.

articles, and works of literature and art, all in one fell swoop."[13]

Led by the American Civil Liberties Union, a coalition of groups filed a complaint asking the United States District Court for the Eastern District of Pennsylvania to stop the CDA from going into effect. The American Library Association filed a separate complaint. The combined plaintiffs (those who brought the complaint) included Planned Parenthood, Stop Prisoner Rape, the Critical Path AIDS Project, the Freedom to Read Foundation, the Electronic Frontier Foundation, online companies such as America Online and Prodigy, and various writers, publishers, and other groups.

Government Cannot Limit Global Conversation

The three-judge panel that heard the case found the CDA was both "vague" and "overbroad." The law was vague because people would have trouble figuring out what they could—or could not—say on the Internet. The CDA was overbroad because it would restrict lawful conduct. In other words, people might avoid talking about AIDS prevention, abortion, or other sexually related issues for fear of breaking the law.

Judge Stewart Dalzell, in a separate written opinion, talked about the Internet as a new medium that deserved the same protection as the printed word. He said, "As the most participatory form of speech yet developed, the Internet deserves the highest protection from governmental intrusion."[14]

The Battle Continues

The government wanted to prove that the CDA was constitutional. Under Attorney General Janet Reno, the U.S. Justice Department appealed the case to the Supreme Court. The Justice Department based much of its argument on three prior cases restricting freedom of speech.

The first was *Ginsberg* v. *New York*. In the 1968 *Ginsberg* ruling, the Court had upheld a New York statute forbidding the sale of obscene magazines to minors. (However, parents could show the magazines to their children if they wished.)[15]

FCC v. *Pacifica* was the second case. In 1978, the Court had banned indecent speech in over-the-air broadcasts during certain periods of the day. One reason was to protect children who might overhear the broadcast. The Justice Department argued that *Pacifica* set a precedent for restricting speech on the Internet.[16]

The third case cited was *Renton* v. *Playtime Theatres*. In the 1986 *Renton* case, the Supreme Court had supported a zoning ordinance that allowed the city of Renton, Washington, to keep sexually graphic "adult films" away from family neighborhoods.[17] The Justice Department said the CDA would create similar zones on the Internet.

Everyone a Town Crier

The Supreme Court did not completely dismiss the government's argument. Protecting children was a legitimate government interest, said the Court. They also agreed the Internet included inappropriate material for minors.

However, the Court was not persuaded by the government's examples. Robert S. Peck writes,

> The statute, [the Court] concluded, was not like an "obscene for minors" law, was not like the prohibition on broadcast indecency and was not another form of zoning regulation, concentrating similar businesses in a single location. In fact, the CDA covered a far greater range of communications than these types of laws, with potentially unsettling results for free speech in the twenty-first century.[18]

He points out that the justices found many differences between the CDA and the laws and rulings in three cases cited by the Justice Department. For example, the *Ginsberg* ruling in 1968 had allowed parents to decide what their children would see. By contrast, the CDA would not allow parents to choose material for children. In fact, under the CDA,

> a parent allowing her 17-year-old to use the family computer to obtain information on the Internet that she, in her parental judgement, deems appropriate could face a lengthy prison term.[19]

As for the 1978 *Pacifica* ruling, indecent speech was limited to certain times of the day. Unlike *Pacifica*, the CDA would operate at all hours. Another reason *Pacifica* did not apply to the Internet, according to the Supreme Court, was the difference between the two forms of media. To find information, Internet users performed a series of steps. They

The Supreme Court has reviewed many laws dealing with limits on freedom of speech.

were not likely to come across "a sexually explicit site by accident." However, an indecent broadcast could "invade" the home if someone had a radio or television set turned on.[20]

Finally, the Supreme Court did not think the *Renton* ruling of 1986 offered support for censoring the Internet. *Renton* was designed to protect property values by keeping sexually oriented businesses away from family neighborhoods. Yet *Renton* did not restrict the message or content of the adult movies. The Court realized that the CDA would restrict certain types of speech throughout "the entire universe of cyberspace."[21]

On June 26, 1997, the Supreme Court struck down

the Communications Decency Act. The Court cited many reasons for its decision. No technology existed to protect minors from indecent communications in chat rooms, through e-mail, or on nonprofit sites without also denying adults their rights to protected speech. The CDA covered not only commercial speech but also nonprofit groups and private individuals. The law would have criminalized material with serious social value, such as discussions of prison rape.

Writing for the Court, Justice John Paul Stevens praised the Internet as an important new form of mass communication that allowed the average person to be both a listener and a speaker:

> This dynamic, multifaceted category of communication includes not only traditional print and news services, but also audio, video, and still images, as well as interactive, real-time dialogue. Through the use of chat rooms, any person with a phone line can become a town crier with a voice that resonates farther than it could from any soapbox.[22]

The Child Online Protection Act

Soon Congress made a second attempt to clean up cyberspace with the Child Online Protection Act, or COPA. Some people called it "the son of the CDA," because this law also tried to keep children from finding online porn.

Those who drafted the law studied the Supreme Court's decision in the CDA. They tried to avoid the same mistakes. COPA differed from the CDA in three important ways. The law applied only to material on the World Wide Web and not to other services, such as e-mail. Only commercial pornographers—those who charged a fee for sexually explicit materials—were targeted. Finally, COPA used a more precise legal definition to describe objectionable materials. COPA regulated content that is "harmful to minors."[23] Previous laws have held that "harmful to minors" materials can be restricted.

Companies that posted sexually explicit material had to establish credit card verification systems or other means to stop minors from entering the site. The penalty for transmitting illegal material to under-age recipients was a jail term of up to six months, a $50,000 fine, or both.

President Clinton signed COPA into law on October 21, 1998. A coalition of groups led by the ACLU immediately challenged the law. The plaintiffs were mostly Web site operators who published materials on sexual health, "visual art and poetry," or resources for gays and lesbians.[24] The plaintiffs said their material was useful for adults but might be considered "harmful to minors" by some communities. Because they made money from their Web sites, they worried they could be prosecuted under the new law.

The U.S. District Court for the Eastern District of Pennsylvania heard the case. Ruling in favor of the plaintiffs, the district court granted a preliminary injunction that stopped the government from putting the law into effect. The government appealed to a higher court. When the case reached the United States Court of Appeals for the Third Circuit Court, a new argument took center stage. *Who* decides what is harmful?

Community Standards in Cyberspace

COPA relied on the legal definition of "harmful to minors." The harmful-to-minors standard is like the legal definition of obscenity, except that minors are the target audience rather than adults, according to the National Law Center for Children and Families. Under this guideline, a judge and jury must decide if a book, magazine, film, painting, or other work, "taken as a whole," is obscene for people seventeen or younger.

Courts base their decision on the community standards test, among other criteria. They ask if the controversial material violates the jury's standards of acceptability. This is not difficult to do in a geographical community. Local citizens can decide if a work appeals to a prurient, or unwholesome, interest in sex.

But how could people make a similar determination about a Web site? In cyberspace, a Web site can attract visitors from all over the world. Opponents charged that COPA would allow conservative communities to impose their standards on more liberal ones.[25] For instance, for fear of breaking the law, a Web site based in a California community might edit its content to please a conservative community in Alabama.

Defenders of COPA put forth a different concept of community. They defined the standards of the adult community in general terms. Bruce Taylor, who helped draft the law, explains how a community standard could be applied to cyberspace. Whether the case deals with Internet porn or mail or video porn, the jury still decides how the average adult would judge the material. He says:

> A jury is told they can consider the views of average adults in the community to arrive at the viewpoint of the "average adult person." This is not a geographic view as much as a general adult population standard that is applied—and that standard is virtually the same all over when it comes to hard-core pornography.[26]

On June 23, 2000, the Court of Appeals agreed with the plaintiffs that the community standards component of COPA would unfairly restrict Web speakers. They kept the ban on COPA in place.

Next to hear the case was the Supreme Court. On May 13, 2002, the Court ruled on the issue of community standards on the Internet. The Court held that "COPA's reliance on 'community standards' to

Abbreviations

ACLU—American Civil Liberties Union

AUP—acceptable use policy

CDA—Communications Decency Act

CIPA—Children's Internet Protection Act

COPA—Child Online Protection Act

COPPA—Children's Online Privacy Protection Act

FCC—Federal Communications Commission

NRC—National Research Council

identify what is 'harmful to minors' does not by itself render the statute . . . overbroad for First Amendment purposes."[27]

Writing for the Court, Justice Clarence Thomas wrote, "If a publisher chooses to send its material into a particular community . . . it is the publisher's responsibility to abide by that community's standards."[28]

However, the Supreme Court still refused to let COPA take effect, and it did not address whether the law was unconstitutional on other grounds. Instead, the Court sent back the case to a lower court for review. As of this writing, the fate of COPA is still unknown. Although the community standards issue has been resolved, critics say the law may still be overturned for other reasons.

Censoring Schools and Libraries

The most recent law affecting schools and libraries was the Children's Internet Protection Act (CIPA). CIPA required schools and libraries to put technology-protection measures such as filters on their computer networks. CIPA said libraries and schools could lose federal funds unless they kept minors from finding visual depictions of obscenity, child pornography, and harmful-to-minors material on the Internet. Adults in public libraries could not use library computers to find obscenity or child pornography.

President Clinton signed CIPA into law on December 21, 2000. By the following month, the ACLU and other groups had filed lawsuits. One of the plaintiffs was the American Library Association.

5

Libraries and the First Amendment

On March 25, 2002, a federal district court in Philadelphia heard the challenge to CIPA led by the American Library Association. Two months later, on May 31, the three-judge court overturned the provision that forced libraries to use filters or else lose a source of federal funding.

After a careful examination of filtering technology, the court concluded:

> Thousands of Web pages containing protected speech are wrongly blocked by the four leading filtering programs and these pages represent only a fraction of Web pages wrongly blocked by the programs.[1]

44

Not only did filters over-block useful and legal information, but they allowed some inappropriate content to reach users.[2] The Justice Department appealed the case.

Technology Tools

Blocking and filtering systems limit what you can find on the Internet. Filters screen out large quantities of pornographic material. Users can choose to exclude other types of information, too. These include advertisements, information about criminal skills, drugs, gambling, alcohol, tobacco, and so on.

Filtering products work on home computers or on computer networks at schools, libraries, or other organizations. Many Internet service providers offer blocking services to subscribers, so that objectionable material never reaches the end user.

Filters use one or more technologies to restrict forbidden content. One approach is to use lists of Internet addresses to steer where you go online. Lists may be of either approved sites (called "white" lists) or of prohibited addresses (called "black" lists). Software manufacturers typically keep these addresses secret because list development is costly and they do not want competitors to use the information.[3]

Another approach is to use keyword blocking. Keyword blocking can keep a search engine from returning answers to a query, if that query contains suspect words, such as "sex" or "Satan." Early versions of keyword blocking sometimes stopped people from finding innocent material, such as information on breast cancer. Software manufacturers claim that newer, more sophisticated products do a better job of avoiding these errors.[4]

A third capability built into popular Web browsers and other programs is label recognition. Labeling and rating systems depend on having someone assign a label to a Web site. Either the Web site publisher or another person does this. The label tells users about the content. (Movies are rated according to content, too, and given designations such as G for general audiences or R for restricted viewing. Web site labeling resembles this practice.) Unlike other filtering technologies, labeling and rating systems allow people to know exactly what is being blocked. To date, not enough of the Web has been labeled for this approach to be widely used.[5]

Image analysis filters block sexually explicit pictures. Industry expert Lorrie Faith Cranor of AT&T Research Labs says these products can often do a fairly good job of recognizing human nudity, but are less adept at recognizing pornographic cartoons or people using drugs.[6]

Some filters track conversations in chat rooms and e-mail correspondence. Others can keep you from giving out personal information on the Internet.

Filters Over-block and Under-block

An article that appeared in the *Dayton Daily News* illustrated one of the problems with filters. After months of work, the staff of the Flesh Public Library

One type of technology used to filter Web sites is label recognition. These systems assign a rating, similar to the motion picture rating system, to show which sites are suitable for kids.

in Piqua, Ohio, gathered to see their new Web site. However, the library director could not access the library's home page.

He soon discovered why: The filtering system on the library's computer had blocked the Web site. According to the account in the newspaper, the computer had objected to the word "flesh" linked with "public."

"We banned ourselves," the director reportedly told his staff.[7]

As shown by the problem of the seventy-year-old library, named after businessman Leo Flesh, filters can block legal and useful information.

A 2001 study examined four popular filtering programs used in public libraries. Out of five hundred thousand sites tested, more than four thousand were blocked erroneously. In other words, the sites contained legal and appropriate information.[8]

Over-blocking happens for several reasons. Rapidly changing information on the Internet contributes to

Protecting children in schools and libraries was the intent of the Children's Internet Protection Act, which required the use of computer filters. The American Library Association and the ACLU opposed the law.

the problem. Once a software company puts a Web site on a forbidden list, that address can be blocked indefinitely, even if the content changes. Software companies may not have time to re-review addresses that have already been classified.[9]

Sometimes an entire Web site is blocked because of a single page. For example, suppose a magazine's Web site posts articles about safe sex, career advancement, hairstyles, and spring decorating. Some filters might block all of the articles because of the column on sex.

Differences of opinion may account for some over-blocking. Software vendors may think families and certain clients want a particular type of site blocked and so will err on the side of caution.

On the other hand, filters cannot block all objectionable material on the Internet. *Consumer Reports* tested leading software filters in 2001. All filters tested, except for one, allowed "20 percent of the objectionable sites through in their entirety."[10]

Protecting Patrons From Unwanted Materials

CIPA required public libraries to use filtered access on all computers, including those used by adults. Yet rather than use filtering, the federal district court identified several other ways libraries could protect patrons while avoiding First Amendment concerns. The court encouraged libraries to enforce Internet use policies and to involve parents in their children's online activities. Libraries could place terminals used by minors in high-traffic areas to discourage inappropriate behavior. Libraries could also offer filters to parents and others who wanted them.[11] At the time of the trial, most public libraries were already using one or more of these techniques.

Public Debate Not Over

Despite overturning CIPA's requirement for libraries, the three-judge panel in Philadelphia said they were "sympathetic" to the lawmakers who passed the act. Congress wanted people to reap the benefits of the Internet without being subjected to obscenity or having children exposed to harmful-to-minors material, the court said.[12]

Strong support for CIPA also came from young people. In 2001, the Kaiser Family Foundation surveyed a group of students aged fifteen to twenty-four years old. Two thirds of those surveyed approved of CIPA's goals.[13]

A Decisive Victory for Lawmakers

To the surprise of many, the Supreme Court reversed the judgment of the U.S. District Court for the Eastern District of Pennsylvania. On June 23, 2003, by a vote of six to three, the Court upheld the government's right to enforce CIPA.

The Court said CIPA did not cause libraries "to violate the Constitution."[14] Nor did CIPA "penalize" libraries that chose not to use filters. As Chief Justice William Rehnquist explained, "To the extent that libraries wish to offer unfiltered access, they are free to do so without federal assistance."[15] In other words, Congress did not want to pay for a library's Internet access if that library used unfiltered computers. The Court said the government had the right to do this.

The Court also looked at how easily people could get information in spite of filtering software. Librarians could disable filters for adults doing legitimate research, under the provisions of CIPA. The district court had said patrons might be too embarrassed to ask a librarian to unblock a site. Disagreeing with the lower court, Justice Rehnquist said, "The Constitution does not guarantee the right to acquire information at a public library without any risk of embarrassment."[16]

Many people were disappointed by the Court's decision. Kevin Bankston, an attorney for the Electronic Frontier Foundation (EFF), called the decision "a tremendous blow to the free speech rights of child and adult library patrons and Internet publishers."[17]

The American Library Association called on filtering companies to provide more information about the blocking process and to reveal the criteria they used. Promising to research and evaluate filtering products, the ALA said it would support libraries as "they struggle with this very difficult decision."[18]

Librarians Who Support Filters

Although the ALA was dismayed by the Court's ruling, not all librarians object to filters. As of 2002, 7 percent of the nation's nine thousand public libraries used filters on all their terminals. Nearly 17 percent of libraries nationwide used filters on some or all of their Internet computers.[19]

Filters are effective aids to prevent young people from searching for pornography, says librarian David Biek of the Tacoma Public Library. Biek told the National Research Council (NRC) that young patrons in his library made "28,000 attempts to access sexually explicit materials" in 2000. Biek concluded:

> Many young people are not making "good choices" in their use of the Internet and it is debatable whether classes and tips offered by the library will affect this. Mostly, these Internet users are young teens, on their own in the after-school hours, in family situations that do not include the provision of other activities in other places during this time.[20]

Other librarians testified to the NRC that filters removed "political pressure." In other words, members of the community were less likely to complain about pornography in the library or to worry about their children when computers were filtered.[21]

Some librarians told the NRC that they support filters because they feel uncomfortable confronting patrons who are viewing sexually explicit material in the library.[22] A librarian in Chicago filed a grievance against the Chicago Public Library in 2001 for allowing patrons to use unfiltered computers. She claimed pornography on the Internet created "a hostile work environment."[23]

Sued for Using Filters

Controversy over filters did not begin with CIPA. Since the mid-1990s, American public libraries have struggled to sort out filtering issues. In 1997, local citizens sued the Loudoun County Library board in Virginia. The library board had voted to install filters in the public library. Some citizens became upset.

Three days before Christmas, a group of parents, teachers, and other citizens filed a legal complaint. Loudoun patrons argued that filters kept them from finding constitutionally protected material. *Mainstream Loudoun* v. *Loudoun County Library Board* was the first lawsuit of its kind aimed at public libraries.

During the trial, attorneys for the plaintiffs produced a list of information blocked by the library's filtering product. The list included valuable sites such as Banned Books Online at Carnegie Mellon University, the American Association of University Women in Maryland, the articles of newspaper columnist Rob Morse of the *San Francisco Examiner*, and the works of Mexican artist and singer Sergio Arau.[24] Feminist issues, sex education, and gay and lesbian discussions were blocked, along with other useful public information.

Loudoun library patrons said that filtering the Internet was like removing articles from a set of encyclopedias. Library board members saw their actions differently. They argued that filtering was the same as not acquiring an objectionable book for the library's collection.

Judge Leonie M. Brinkema, a former librarian,

heard the case. She agreed with the Loudoun library patrons. In her decision, she wrote that the library board had "misconstrued the nature of the Internet."[25] She concluded that the Internet was indeed like a set of encyclopedias from which the library board had removed "portions deemed unfit for library patrons."[26] To support her opinion, she cited an important case involving free speech in the school library.

Book Banning in the Library

In 1982, the Supreme Court examined a case called the *Board of Education, Island Trees School Union Free School District No. 26* v. *Pico*. A New York school board had removed ten books from a high school library because they considered the books to be "anti-American, anti-Christian, anti-Semitic, and just plain filthy." The banned books included *Slaughterhouse-Five, The Naked Ape*, and *Down These Mean Streets*.[27]

A group of students and their families sued the board of education for violating their First Amendment right to receive information and ideas. The Supreme Court acknowledged that school library boards play "a substantial, legitimate role" in selecting books. Nevertheless, the Court ruled in favor of the students. Writing for the plurality of the Court (four justices, with whom a fifth justice voted, though on slightly different grounds), Justice William Brennan affirmed the protection of books in the school library:

Local school boards may not remove books from school library shelves simply because they dislike the ideas contained in those books and seek by their removal to "prescribe what shall be orthodox in politics, nationalism, religion, or other matters of opinion."[28]

In the *Island Trees* case, the Court decided it was unacceptable to remove books from a school library because some people found the ideas offensive. In the *Loudoun* case, Judge Brinkema held that the First Amendment also limits a public library's ability to

These books were removed from the library at Island Trees High School because the school board considered them "filthy." However, the Supreme Court ruled that the action violated students' First Amendment rights.

block access to "constitutionally protected materials within its collection."[29]

Libraries in the Middle

Not long after citizens sued the Loudoun County Library board for using filters, a California parent sued a library for not using them. In 1998, the mother of a young boy filed a complaint against the city of Livermore for allowing her son to download pornographic images at the library.

A judge dismissed the case. However, the incident shows why some libraries might feel caught in the middle of the censorship debate. Libraries and courts have had to think deeply about the pros and cons of filters. In spite of the Supreme Court's ruling to uphold CIPA, not all the justices agreed it was the right thing to do. Justice David Souter, in a dissenting opinion, wrote:

> Quite simply, we can smell a rat when a library blocks material already in its control, just as we do when a library removes books from its shelves for reasons having nothing to do with wear and tear, obsolescence, or lack of demand.[30]

Elsewhere, he wrote, "There is no good reason, then, to treat blocking of adult enquiry as anything different from the censorship it presumptively is."[31]

6

Schools, Free Speech, and the Web

Students use the Internet at school in many ways. A virtual field trip to the tombs of ancient Egypt makes a history lesson more fun. Students and teachers can connect with peers at other schools or find experts to answer questions. Using the Internet also helps students master technological skills. By 2000, nearly all public schools had Internet access.[1]

Teachers use the Internet to research lesson plans, particularly in social studies, history, and science.[2] By 2001, 75 percent of public schools maintained Web sites where they posted information such as school calendars, program guidelines, school rules, and news about sports and club activities.[3]

Although a valuable resource, the Internet has caused problems for a small number of school administrators and students. The trouble arises over online behavior. Rules for behavior at school are typically well defined. Defying administrators, publicly ridiculing fellow students, and threatening teachers are unacceptable at most schools. But what if a student does these activities at home on a private Web site? Can schools discipline students under such circumstances?

Off-Campus Web Sites Raise Questions

During the 1990s, a handful of off-campus Web sites caught the public's attention. Students created Web pages at home that disturbed school administrators. Controversial Web sites criticized teachers, school policies, and classmates. Some contained threatening words.

While a junior at Woodland High School in eastern Missouri, Brandon Beussink created a contentious off-campus Web site in 1998. The seventeen-year-old student described his teachers and school in vulgar terms and provided a link to the school's home page.[4] When the principal discovered the site, he suspended Beussink for ten days.

The student failed four classes because of his unexcused absences. He then sued the school for violating his First Amendment right to freedom of speech.[5]

U.S. District Judge Rodney W. Sippel granted a preliminary injunction, or ruling, in support of the student. The judge said the school could not use Beussink's suspension to calculate his grades, nor could school officials force the student to remove his Web page. Judge Sippel wrote: "Disliking or being upset by the content of a student's speech is not an acceptable justification for limiting student speech. . . ."[6]

According to the Student Press Law Center, most students have successfully defended their right to criticize school officials on Web sites created at home.[7] However, schools *can* discipline students when online speech is disruptive.

Consider the 1998 case of a Pennsylvania eighth grader who threatened to kill his math teacher. On the boy's home-based Web site was a gruesome image of the teacher, according to an article published by the National Education Association. The teacher was decapitated and bleeding from the neck. The student posted the question, "Why Should She Die?" and listed his reasons. Visitors were asked to help pay for a hit man.[8]

More than two hundred people saw the site. The teacher became so distraught that she took a leave of absence for the remainder of the school year. Her health problems caused her to retire after twenty-six years of teaching.[9]

School officials expelled the eighth-grader. Although the boy and his family sued the school, saying his free speech rights had been violated, the Commonwealth Court of Pennsylvania ruled in favor of the school. The court decided that the Web site had disrupted classroom activities. A jury later awarded the teacher $500,000 in damages.[10]

To be a responsible online speaker, you should keep a few guidelines in mind, cautions Nancy Willard, research associate at the Responsible Netizen Institute in Eugene, Oregon. Willard urges young Internet users to cultivate responsible speech practices. Students sometimes mistakenly believe they are totally anonymous online, says Willard. They may also find it easier to be cruel because they cannot see the other person's face.

A better approach, according to Willard, is to focus on issues rather than individuals. "To be an effective agent of change, you must learn not to attack people," she says.[11]

How Courts Handle Off-Campus Web Sites

The case of a Washington State student explains how many courts look at off-campus Web sites. Karl Beidler made fun of the assistant principal on a private Web site.[12] Using photos from an old school album, the student portrayed the assistant principal as a Nazi and posted lewd and vulgar statements.[13] The boy was quickly expelled. He later sued the school, claiming his First Amendment rights had been violated.

In July 2000, the case went before Judge William Thomas McPhee of the Thurston County Superior Court of Washington. Judge McPhee reviewed several court decisions made years before the widespread

Most public schools in the United States now have Internet access. Students can use the Internet to master skills, perform research, and connect with others.

use of the Web. One was a 1979 case called *Thomas v. Board of Education, Granville Central School District*.

Who Controls Off-Campus Newspapers?

In the *Thomas* case, several high school students had published a newspaper off campus containing sexually explicit language. Classmates could purchase the paper near the school grounds for a nickel. One day a teacher took away a student's copy. School officials punished the student publishers who, in turn, filed a lawsuit.

The case was decided by the U.S. Court of Appeals. Writing for the court, Chief Judge Irving Kaufman ruled in favor of the students. He said school officials could not control activities "beyond the schoolhouse gate."[14] Judge Kaufman wrote, "When an educator seeks to extend his dominion beyond these bounds . . . he must answer to the same constitutional commands that bind all other institutions of government."[15]

No Authority "Beyond the Schoolhouse Gate"

In the Beidler case, the judge suggested that the same principles that had guided the court's decision in *Thomas* still applied to off-campus student speech, even though society and technology had changed. "Today the first amendment protects students' speech to the same extent as in 1979 or in 1969, when the U.S. Supreme Court decided *Tinker* v. *Des Moines*," wrote Judge McPhee.[16]

The second case cited by Judge McPhee in his ruling was *Tinker* v. *Des Moines Independent Community School District*. The *Tinker* decision was a landmark ruling by the Supreme Court protecting student expression at school.

A Victory for Students

During the 1960s, many people disagreed with the government's involvement in the Vietnam War. In December of 1965, a small group met at the home of a Des Moines, Iowa, family to plan a peaceful protest of the war. Several students planned to wear black armbands to school to show support for a truce.

Local school officials heard about the plan. On December 14, 1965, they quickly passed a school regulation banning armbands. Two days later, John Tinker, his sister Mary Beth, and Christopher Eckhardt wore their armbands anyway. School officials suspended the three teenagers.

The families filed a lawsuit, and the case eventually reached the Supreme Court. The Court ruled in favor of the students. Wearing armbands was a form of speech and not a disruptive activity that threatened the school environment, said the Court. Furthermore, students did not "shed their constitutional rights to freedom of speech or expression at the schoolhouse gate."[17]

On the other hand, students could not disrupt classwork, cause disorder, or invade the rights of others. Schools could discipline students for a genuine disruption. However, they could not stifle free speech for fear a disruption might occur.[18]

Writing for the majority, Justice Abe Fortas said:

> Any word spoken, in class, in the lunchroom, or on the campus, that deviates from the views of another person may start an argument or cause a disturbance. But our Constitution says that we must take this risk . . . and our history says that it is this sort of hazardous freedom—this kind of openness— that is the basis of our national strength and of the independence and vigor of Americans who grow up and live in this relatively permissive, often disputatious, society.[19]

Tinker Applies to Web Sites

In the Beidler case in 2000, attorneys for the Thurston School District argued that Karl Beidler's Web site disrupted classroom activities. However, Judge McPhee found that Beidler's Web site did not disrupt classroom activities or affect school discipline. Therefore, school officials had no right to punish the student.[20]

"Schools can and will adjust to the new challenges created by such students and the Internet, but not at the expense of the First Amendment," wrote Judge McPhee.[21]

Attorneys for the North Thurston School District pointed to two other landmark cases giving administrators authority to control the school environment. *Bethel School District No. 403* v. *Fraser* granted

In 1965, Mary Beth Tinker and two other students were suspended from school for wearing black armbands to protest the Vietnam War. But the Supreme Court found that they had a right to wear the armbands, since this is a form of symbolic speech—and students have the right to free speech if it does not disrupt the school environment.

schools authority to discipline students for vulgar language. *Hazelwood School District* v. *Kuhlmeier* gave officials the right to censor the content of student newspapers.

No Vulgar Language

In the mid-1980s, high school student Matthew Fraser nominated a fellow student for a school election. Fraser used sexually suggestive language that violated the school's code of conduct. Officials suspended him from school for three days. Fraser sued.

When *Bethel School District No. 403* v. *Fraser* reached the Supreme Court, the justices ruled in favor of the Bethel school district. Chief Justice Warren Burger noted a difference between Fraser's lewd language and political speech upheld in the *Tinker* ruling. The Court said that vulgar language was inappropriate in a public school setting.

The Court also said that the freedom to voice controversial views in the classroom must be balanced against "society's countervailing interest in teaching students the boundaries of appropriate behavior."[22] The *Fraser* ruling gave school officials more authority to govern sexually explicit student speech on campus.

A Victory for School Officials

School-sponsored newspapers came to the Court's attention in the 1988 case of *Hazelwood School District* v. *Kuhlmeier*.

Three student journalists worked on a high school newspaper in St. Louis, Missouri. The principal pulled two stories from the newspaper shortly before it went to press. One story was about pregnant teens. The other discussed divorce and its impact on students. Both stories were true, and they used quotations from students at the high school. Even though people's names were not used in the articles, the principal believed those individuals could be identified. He worried that they might feel uncomfortable.

When the case reached the Supreme Court, the justices supported the school principal. Justice Byron White ruled that schools could refuse to publish material contrary to the school's educational mission, even if the material did not create a disruption in the classroom. School officials could avoid promoting views that created controversy for the school. Schools could also refuse to publish materials that did not meet educational standards. The ruling applied to school newspapers, school plays, and extracurricular activities paid for by the school.[23]

Hazelwood School District v. *Kuhlmeier* gave administrators more authority to edit school-based publications.

Off-Campus Web Site Governed Differently

Attorneys for the North Thurston School District argued that *Fraser* and *Kuhlmeier* gave the principal the right to discipline Beidler.

Judge McPhee disagreed. He ruled that Beidler's off-campus Web site had First Amendment protection. Although Beidler also used "highly offensive,

'Beat It, Kids — This Show Is For Adults Only'

Many newspapers criticized the Supreme Court's decision in the Hazelwood case.

vulgar, sexually explicit and lewd" language on his Web site, his case was not like *Fraser*.[24] Matthew Fraser had addressed an audience in a school setting. His listeners had no choice but to hear his words. By contrast, Beidler's Web site could be avoided by anyone who wished to do so.

Nor did the *Kuhlmeier* decision apply to Beidler's case, said the judge. A Web site created off campus differs from a newspaper published in a journalism class. Beidler's site was not connected to a classroom activity.

Students and the Bill of Rights

Beidler's case was one of several in the 1990s involving conflicts between school officials and students who created Web sites at home. As a general rule, schools do not have authority to discipline students for off-campus Web sites unless school officials can prove that the sites cause disruptions in the classroom, interfere with lesson plans, or invade the rights of others, explains David Hudson, staff attorney with the First Amendment Center at Vanderbilt University.[25]

Hudson writes that if a student's Web site was created as part of the school curriculum or on school computers, administrators might have more of a case for exercising discipline.[26] However, he observes, "Students are citizens who should also enjoy the protections of the Bill of Rights, particularly when they are in the privacy of their own homes."[27]

How Schools Protect Students Online

Schools use multiple measures to keep students safe during the school day. By 2002, 78 percent of school districts surveyed relied on teachers to supervise online activities and nine out of ten districts had installed filtering software on school computers.[28] Filters are now the primary way schools censor the Web. Filters regulate online use in a number of ways. Some limit the amount of time a student is on the Internet. Others block out controversial material. Filters can keep students from visiting chat rooms or newsgroups or from giving out sensitive information such as their address. School administrators can decide which categories to block. Authorized people can also override or unblock a site, if needed.

At more than half of school districts surveyed (58 percent), students had to obey a code of honor when using the Internet in 2002. Nearly one in five districts (19 percent) had acceptable use policies (AUPs).[29]

A typical AUP states the terms and conditions of using the Internet. The policy outlines rules for behavior and safety guidelines. Students are reminded of penalties if they fail to honor the contract. Most AUPs require the signatures of students and parents.

An Ongoing Debate

Schools and students continue to debate freedom of speech offline and in cyberspace. Filters are controversial in schools as in libraries, although no one has yet mounted a legal challenge to classroom filters. Nevertheless, many free speech advocates oppose the blocking of constitutionally protected material in a classroom environment. Critics say that filters deprive students of the opportunity to develop needed skills for navigating the Internet safely. How, they ask, can students become responsible online citizens unless they are given the opportunity to exercise their judgment? Both students and schools test the boundaries of the law because of differing interpretations of freedom of speech. Schools clamp down on activities when they threaten (or seem to threaten) the stability of the school environment. Students challenge rules they believe to be unfair.

The Internet amplifies this conflict. Students, teachers, and administrators are still discovering how to best use the Internet.

7

Online Pornography and Other Controversies

In 1873, Anthony Comstock founded the New York Society for the Suppression of Vice. His work laid the foundation for today's postal regulations on obscenity. Under the Comstock Law, prosecutors destroyed "134,000 pounds of books of 'improper character.'"[1] Comstock was named postmaster general, and he took up the cause of fighting pornography in America.

Society has become more lenient since the 1800s, but people still wrestle with fundamental questions. Are pornographic images and stories harmful to society? Do they cause social misbehavior? How does one draw the line between indecency, which is protected by the First Amendment, and obscenity, which is not protected?

Protected and Unprotected Speech

Not all forms of speech enjoy First Amendment protection. The Supreme Court has ruled that *fighting words* (those intended to cause acts of violence by the persons to whom they are directed) are outside the bounds of the law. Another prohibited form of speech is *libel*, which means publishing information that is untrue in an effort to destroy someone's reputation or standing in the community.

Obscenity also falls outside the protection of the First Amendment. In broad terms, obscenity is a form of pornography without social value. The Supreme Court examined the issue of "hard-core" or extreme pornography in 1957, in a case known as *Roth* v. *United States*.

Samuel Roth, a bookseller in New York, had sent advertisements through the mail to solicit business for his pornographic publications. He was convicted of obscenity under a New York statute. The Supreme Court upheld Roth's conviction.

Delivering the Court's opinion, Justice Brennan said the First Amendment was not intended to "protect every utterance" and that obscenity was "outside the protection intended for speech and press." He added that obscenity has been seen as "utterly without redeeming social importance" for most of our nation's history.[2]

Anthony Comstock, who founded the New York Society for the Suppression of Vice in 1873, was a crusader against "improper" books.

The Supreme Court tried to give a more precise definition of obscenity in 1973 in the case of *Miller v. California*. A bookseller mailed out sexually explicit brochures advertising five books, including one called *The History of Pornography*. A restaurant manager and his mother in Newport Beach, California, received one of the mailings and contacted the police. A lawsuit ensued.

When the case reached the Supreme Court, the court established a new standard for obscenity. A book, movie, magazine, or other work was legally obscene if it met all three of the following conditions: (a) "the average person" using "community standards" would find that the work, taken as a whole, appealed to an unwholesome interest in sex; (b) the work described sexual conduct in a patently, or extremely, offensive way; and (c) the work, "taken as a whole, lacks serious literary, artistic, political, or scientific value."[3]

The Court said that "our Nation is simply too big and too diverse" for a federal court to define obscenity for every community.[4] So the Court allowed individual communities, using state laws, to decide if a work went beyond people's collective standard of decency.

The ruling in the *Miller* case gave communities a tool to evaluate sexually explicit works. However, confusion still exists over the meaning of the word "pornography." In 1986, the U.S. Attorney General's Commission on Pornography said pornography means "sexually explicit" materials that create lust in the viewer.[5] People often use the word loosely to mean anything they find offensive, whether it meets the legal definition of obscenity or not. Another meaning of pornography comes from feminists who define it as material that portrays women in a degrading way.

Not all feminists object to pornography. Some argue that censorship is far more dangerous than pornography. According to this view, the power to limit sexual expression could be used to limit any unpopular belief, including women's rights.[6]

Attitudes Toward Sexually Explicit Materials

Attitudes toward sexually explicit materials differ. At one end of the spectrum are free speech advocates who often defend provocative material for the same reason they defend any sort of controversial speech. They believe that people in a free society should have the right to choose what they want to read, receive, or create. The ACLU says, "Censorship is like poison gas: a powerful weapon that can harm you when the wind shifts."[7]

Former Supreme Court justice Oliver Wendell Holmes said,

> If there is any principle of the Constitution that more imperatively calls for attachment than any other it is the principle of free thought—not free thought for those who agree with us but freedom for the thought we hate.[8]

The purpose of the First Amendment is to protect the free exchange of ideas in a democratic society, say civil libertarians. To preserve freedom of expression, the judicial system must tolerate material that offends or even outrages the mainstream public. Another important constitutional concept, according to ACLU president Nadine Strossen, is that the government must see a "clear and present" danger to society to justify censoring speech. Thus, the government may not restrict speech because of its content or message without a compelling reason.[9]

According to the ACLU, "sexually explicit material" functions like other forms of speech by transmitting ideas, promoting self-realization, and serving as a "safety valve" for both the speaker and audience.[10]

Opposing this view are those who see a connection between the consumption of pornography and a host of social ills, including sex crimes against women and children. When the rap group 2 Live Crew was arrested in the late 1980s for obscenity—and later acquitted—columnist George F. Will criticized the media for distorting the issues. Journalists had failed to do accurate reporting, he said. News stories had called the album "provocative" instead of stating the truth.

In Will's opinion, the lyrics of 2 Live Crew's songs glorified sexual violence and cruelty toward women. He compared the brutality described in the song to the 1989 "wilding" attack on a jogger in Central Park that caused the victim to lose most of her blood and left her in a coma. He warned that the "desensitizing of a society will have behavioral consequences."[11]

A 1999 survey suggests that many Americans feel somewhat uncomfortable with pornography or at least uncertain about its effects on society. Slightly more than half those surveyed said they did not agree with the statement "Nude magazines and X-rated movies provide harmless entertainment for those who enjoy it."[12]

Observers say that the Internet offers a new stage for the old pornography debate. Free speech advocates battle attempts to regulate controversial material on the Internet. They worry that rather than protecting children, such regulations will promote government censorship of other types of speech.

Those who believe that pornography harms society in general, and children in particular, want the government to stem the flow of graphic sexual content on the Internet. An opinion poll conducted in 1999 for the Kaiser Family Foundation and Harvard University showed that 78 percent of the public thought "sexually explicit material on the Internet should be regulated" and 57 percent would support a law making it "illegal for a computer network to carry pornographic or adult material."[13]

Prosecuting Obscenity

Communities, states, and the federal government have statutes outlawing obscenity. These laws range from banning topless bars to requiring "adult" theaters to locate away from family neighborhoods.

Federal laws prevent the sexual exploitation of children, prohibit obscene phone calls, and forbid broadcasts of obscene language. Federal laws make it

While most people agree that children should not be exposed to sexually explicit material, they disagree as to how this can best be accomplished.

illegal for anyone to transmit obscenity or child pornography over the Internet.[14]

However, Justice Department prosecutions of obscenity have dwindled since 1992. According to the Transactional Records Access Clearinghouse at Syracuse University, federal prosecutions of obscenity plummeted from forty-two in 1992 to nineteen in 1996 to seven in 2001.[15]

Observers say that during the 1990s, the Justice Department chose not to prosecute commercial pornographers who sold obscenity to adults. Instead, the government pursued child pornographers.

Effects of Viewing Images

Viewing sexual content in the media may affect you in one of several ways, according to the Kaiser Family Foundation. Researchers identify at least four outcomes to measure: You may understand a topic better, have an emotional response to a situation, experience a shift in attitudes, or be encouraged to change your behavior.[16]

Researchers have studied how children respond to sexual themes viewed during prime-time television. The Kaiser Family Foundation report says, "Television and other media can play an important role in educating children and adolescents about sexuality."[17] However, studies suggest only a weak link between TV and real-life sexual behavior, according to Kaiser researchers.[18] Factors more likely to influence a child's behavior include parental involvement, the age of the child, and other issues. Parents can help young people deal with media messages, according to the report. Children viewing television alone are more likely to believe what they see.

The report said, "Given new technologies like the Internet, children will now have access to a wide range of sexual content often in isolated viewing context."[19] No one knows for sure how viewing online pornography may affect young people. Many legal and ethical issues make it difficult to research the topic, according to the report.

The Bomb-Making Controversy

Pornography on the Internet is not the only perceived danger to minors. A tragic event in Colorado sparked a national debate on the dangers of online bomb-making instructions. Details of the following story were reported in the *Rocky Mountain News*. According to the newspaper story, Eric Harris and his friend Dylan Klebold made elaborate plans to set off bombs in their school cafeteria.[20]

On the morning of April 20, 1999, the teenagers walked into the cafeteria of Columbine High School in Littleton, Colorado, and dropped two large duffel bags on the floor. Each bag contained a twenty-pound propane bomb.[21]

Outside the cafeteria, two more bombs were ready to go. The second blast was set to coincide with the arrival of firemen, ambulances, and police, according to investigators.[22]

After dropping the duffel bags, Harris and Klebold went outside to wait. As police later learned, the boys thought a deadly fire would sweep through the cafeteria and engulf their classmates. Harris and Klebold held guns concealed under their coats. They apparently planned to shoot anyone who escaped the fire after the bombs exploded.[23]

But the bombs did not go off inside the cafeteria or in the parking lot. At 11:19 A.M., Harris and Klebold began randomly shooting at classmates.[24] Police called it "the worst school shooting" in the history of the United States.[25] The boys killed a total of twelve students and a teacher and injured twenty-one more young people. At last they took their own lives.[26]

The community and the nation were in shock. As people struggled to make sense of the tragedy, more disturbing news surfaced. More than a year earlier, Harris had published bomb-making instructions on his Web site.[27]

Dangerous Information

After the shooting, investigators searched the school and the homes of the two boys and discovered eighty homemade bombs, said the newspaper.[28]

Several months later, at the Senate Commerce Committee's hearing on Internet filters, people blamed the Internet for contributing to school violence. One witness told the committee, "The Internet offers both propaganda and how-to manuals for those seeking to act out fantasies of intolerance and violence."[29]

Members of the public blamed the Internet, too. A Gallup poll found most people (82 percent) thought the Internet had contributed to the shooting

The tragic events at Columbine led many to reevaluate their beliefs about the kind of information that should be available on the Internet. These students participated in a candlelight vigil to honor the victims of the shootings.

spree. Half of those surveyed said that regulating the Internet could help curb school violence.[30]

In response to the Littleton tragedy, Internet service providers soon announced new tools for parents who wanted to monitor children's whereabouts on the Internet. Popular software filters also block bomb-making information.

Hate Speech on the Net

In 1996, a student at the University of California harassed classmates using the Internet. He sent insulting e-mails to fifty-eight students, most of whom were Asian American.[31] Richard Machado was the first person to be convicted of a hate crime committed on the Internet.

Each year, the Simon Wiesenthal Center in Los Angeles identifies new hate sites. The center tracks Web sites publishing anti-Semitic material. Other problematic sites target homosexuals or promote racial superiority or religious extremism. Some Web sites are tailored to children's interests. The Council of Europe and many other countries regard hate speech as a serious offense.

Although derogatory racial remarks and other forms of hate speech offend many Americans, our free speech traditions protect offensive speech. The First Amendment requires us to be tolerant of hate speech on and off the Internet, according to the Department of Justice. By allowing many points of view, we allow citizens to decide for themselves what is true.[32] According to the department,

> Even where the United States government finds the views expressed to be misguided and repugnant—and surely those are appropriate words to describe racism—our Constitution commands that we neither prohibit nor regulate speech merely because we disapprove of the ideas expressed.[33]

8

Privacy and Predators

Chat rooms, bulletin boards, and e-mail are popular with children, according to a government survey.[1] Many young Internet users also enjoy games, pen pal programs, and contests. In 1998, the government discovered that children were giving away personal information about themselves as they surfed the Web. Young people left their names and e-mail addresses in public places like chat rooms.

Marketers used children's Web sites to collect information about visitors. Some sites sponsored contests with prizes. To enter the contest, children had to fill out forms revealing their names, ages, addresses, and hobbies. Some marketers then sold this information to other companies.

In March 1998, the Federal Trade Commission surveyed 212 commercial children's sites to see if the Web site operators were gathering data about visitors. They found that 188 of the sites were building files of personal information. Only fifty of the sites published privacy policy notices.[2] No more than forty-eight sites told visitors to ask for their parents' permission before giving out information.[3] Three of the sites required children to get a parent's consent first.[4]

To stop this practice, Congress passed the Children's Online Privacy Protection Act in 1998. Online marketers can no longer gather or sell information about children without parental consent. The law covers people under the age of thirteen.

Web sites also collect data about users through a type of information called "cookies." Cookies are legal, but many people are not aware of them as they travel the Internet.

Cookies on the Net

You do not have to give out information about yourself for a system to collect it. Cookies on a given site may be building a picture of you as a consumer.

Internet engineer David Whalen compares them to tickets given out at a laundry cleaner's shop:

> You drop something off, and get a ticket. When you return with the ticket, you get your

clothes back. If you don't have the ticket, then the laundry man doesn't know which clothes are yours.[5]

Whalen and other experts say cookies are harmless messages stored on your computer that are useful to Web site operators. Online sales companies may use cookies to track purchases. Marketers use them to collect information about your preferences.[6] You can set your browser to reject cookies, and many people do this to protect their privacy. However, if you set your browser to reject cookies, there are some sites you cannot visit, since some require that you accept cookies.

A Growing Concern

In 1928, Supreme Court Justice Louis Brandeis observed that advances in science were giving the government new ways to get private information about citizens. He wrote, "Discovery and invention have made it possible for the government. . . to obtain disclosure in court of what is whispered in the closet."[7]

Justice Brandeis argued that the founders of the Constitution never intended to have the government intrude so deeply into our private lives. Rather, said Brandeis, "They conferred . . . the right to be let alone—the most comprehensive of rights and the right most valued by civilized men."[8]

Civil libertarians say this valued right is under attack:

From using the telephone to seeking medical treatment to applying for a job or sending e-mail over the Internet, Americans' right to information privacy is in peril. Our personal and business information is being digitized through an ever-expanding number of computer networks in formats that allow data to be linked, transferred, shared and sold, usually without our knowledge or consent. The same technological advances that have brought enormous benefits to humankind also make us more vulnerable than ever before to unwanted snooping.[9]

Maintaining privacy on the Internet is a growing concern and not just for children. According to the Federal Trade Commission, many people avoid using products and services on the Web because they are afraid of losing their privacy.

Loss of privacy can mean more than inconvenience, especially for children. Predators may use public information to locate their victims. The Department of Justice warns that predators can disguise their identities on the Net. When making new friends online, children may mistakenly believe that they are dealing with other young people and not realize that they are communicating with an adult.

Cyberpredators

She was fourteen and planning a grand adventure. After several years of courting on the Internet, she had a date to meet her "boyfriend" at last. He would drive from Indiana and meet her in a shopping mall in Madison, Wisconsin. They would run away together.

Though many people think they are anonymous on the Internet, some companies use "cookies" to collect information on a user's habits and preferences without the user's being aware of it.

A call to authorities interrupted the plan. Someone who knew the boyfriend contacted CyperTipline, a national hot line maintained by the National Center for Missing and Exploited Children, and asked the staff to investigate. Police soon learned that the boyfriend was a fifty-three-year-old man who had spent time in prison for second-degree murder. He had also been convicted of burglary. The Internet Crimes Against Children Task Force in Wisconsin took over.

Police intercepted the boyfriend at the mall. The man fought so hard to get away that he damaged property. When police searched the man's truck, they found "a 12-inch axe, pieces of rope, Demerol pills, and illegal drug paraphernalia."[10] The man, sentenced to twenty-four years in prison, was a "cyberpredator."

Although opinions differ on whether or not online pornography harms the viewer, people agree that online predators—although small in number—represent a genuine threat. Children can meet dangerous individuals in chat rooms or through e-mail without realizing the true nature of the person. Anonymity gives pedophiles an advantage, says the Department of Justice. However, since 1998, the federal government has made it more difficult for sexual predators to seek out victims online.

J. Robert Flores, administrator of the Office of Juvenile Justice and Delinquency Prevention, says parents cannot assume their children are safe online. "Parents need the same level of commitment to the welfare of their children that a pedophile would invest to gain a child's trust," he explains. He says that a pedophile will spend four hours playing jacks on the floor with a child to win the young person's trust. "The best protection for a child is a loving relationship with responsible adults," says Flores.[11]

The Sexual Predator Punishment Act

Deborah Niemann-Boehle was pleased when the Supreme Court overturned the Communications Decency Act. A Chicago-based journalist and mother, Boehle supported freedom of speech.

However, she also saw the need for laws to protect children after her neighbor posted a message about Niemann-Boehle's nine-year-old daughter on the Internet. The neighbor claimed the child wanted to have sex with men. Soon men began calling the house.

Niemann-Boehle and her husband contacted the local police and the FBI. However, at the time there was no law in place to prohibit the neighbor's actions. As Niemann-Boehle testified before members of Congress:

> This was the beginning of a nightmare that no parents should have to endure. The police advised us to move for two reasons. First, any pedophile in the world could use the reverse directory and maps on the Internet to find our house, and they could come looking for our daughter. She could be raped, abducted or even killed. Second, the person who posted those messages lived across the street from us.[12]

She was one of numerous witnesses who spoke to Congress to help develop the 1998 Child Protection and Sexual Predator Punishment Act. The act made it

Cyberpredators use the Internet to disguise themselves and their intentions. Young users may put themselves in danger if they give away too much information or plan to meet people they do not know.

illegal to contact minors online for sexual purposes or to transmit obscenity to them.

Although the government has passed several laws to safeguard online privacy, experts agree that people must also protect themselves. For children who use the Internet, SafeKids.com suggests several steps to protect privacy. Safety rules posted on the site include the following: Check with your parents before telling anyone you meet online where you live or go to school or how to find your parents at work. Do not send out pictures of yourself unless your parents agree. Never, ever tell anyone—not even your best friend—your Internet password.[13]

The Other Cyberliberty

Privacy protection on the Internet, like freedom of speech, is a source of public debate. People are trying to find ways to protect consumers without making it harder for businesses to operate. Civil libertarians are watching the government carefully to make sure the Internet's power to collect information is not being used to track the movements and activities of citizens.

9

The Global
Debate

Protecting minors from inappropriate content is the focus of the free speech debate in the United States. Many other governments are struggling to control the flow of information over the Net. Political dissent, in particular, troubles repressive governments.

A Tight Rein on the News

Tanks rolled into Tiananmen Square in Beijing, China, in the spring of 1989. Soldiers opened fire on Chinese students filling the Square. The pro-democracy students were protesting government corruption. Hundreds of students were murdered.

A decade later, Webmaster Huang Qi posted information on the Internet about the Tiananmen Square uprising, including details supplied by the mother of one of the victims. She said police had beaten her son to death. Other articles on Huang Qi's Web site dealt with human rights violations against Muslims in the region of Xinjiang.[1]

In the spring of 2001, the Chinese government charged Huang Qi for "subverting state power" and shut down his Web site.[2] Chinese law forbids anyone to publish "news" without permission from government officials.[3] Nor can anyone criticize "the guiding role of Marxism, Leninism, Mao Zedong and Deng Xiaoping's theories," according to a report from the Cato Institute.[4]

Chinese officials forbid access to certain Web sites, according to a 2001 newspaper account. Online monitors remove unacceptable words from chat room conversations. Overseas communications are kept in check with a central filter that prevents Chinese users from visiting certain sites. During 2001, the Chinese government closed down eight thousand Internet cafés where young people could log onto the Web. The cafés reportedly failed to meet government standards of acceptable use.[5]

Controlling Speech on the Internet

China is not the only country eager to control the Web. Press surveys identify fifty-nine countries that have passed laws to restrict freedom of expression online.[6] These countries include Australia, Singapore, France, Saudi Arabia, Italy, and Sweden.

Officials typically object to pornographic materials and sites promoting criminal activities. However, many governments also dislike political criticism. A report from the Cato Institute summarizes some of these practices. For example, Saudi Arabia has a strict code for Internet users. People must resist "any activities violating the social, cultural, political,

In the 1989 demonstrations in Tiananmen Square, Chinese students who protested government corruption were brutally crushed. Truth about the uprising was sent to the world over fax machines, thus sidestepping government censors.

media, economic, and religious values of the Kingdom," according to Council of Ministers Decision 163.[7]

Saudi officials forbid children to visit Pokémon sites. Religious leaders say Pokémon influences the minds of children and promotes gambling.[8]

Sending an overseas e-mail is against the law in Syria, unless you have permission from the government. A violation could land you in jail, says the Cato Institute.[9]

Minors in Australia are barred from unapproved sites. Unsuitable subjects may include "suicide, crime, corruption, marital problems, emotional trauma, drug and alcohol dependency, death and serious illness, racism, and religious issues," according to the Cato Institute.[10]

The World Talks

The United Nations believes in freedom of expression for citizens in every country. In the Universal Declaration of Human Rights, the member nations stated:

> Everyone has the right to freedom of opinion and expression; this right includes the freedom to hold opinions without interference and to seek, receive and impart information and ideas through any means regardless of frontiers.[11]

Governments fear the democratizing power of the Internet, according to online journalist Declan McCullagh, who was one of the plaintiffs in the Communications Decency Act lawsuit. Countries began establishing methods to gain control of online speech in the mid-1990s. McCullagh wrote:

> Governments around the globe are rushing to barricade their borders, dam the flow of foreign data, and create a new world information order. For good reason: an uncensored Net connection can be as deadly to a 20th century government as the plague was three centuries ago . . . the Net carries the virus of freedom.[12]

Internet advocates had hoped the World Wide Web would break down barriers between countries and allow the world's citizens to talk freely. Global efforts to regulate Internet speech discourage many free speech advocates.

However, a 2001 survey by Freedom House offers a brighter view. The report predicts challenges for those who try to influence the Web. As more people go online, "It is reasonable to expect that the Internet will eventually help open most closed societies," said the report.[13]

10

Conflicting Viewpoints and Common Ground

Censorship means restriction of freedom of expression. Governments act as censors when they limit what people can read, say, or do. When Congress passed the Communications Decency Act in 1996, opponents accused the government of trying to censor the Web.

Lawmakers did not describe their actions as censorship. They said they were trying to shield minors from hard-core pornography on the Internet just as young people are protected in geographical communities. However, these goals have proved

99

difficult to achieve in cyberspace without violating the free speech rights of adults. The 2003 ruling on CIPA marked the first time the Supreme Court and Congress have agreed on a method of shielding minors from online porn.

The nature of the Internet has challenged those who want to regulate it. Unlike radio or television, the Internet does not invade someone's home, concluded a federal court. The court also observed that the Internet allows anyone to be a speaker as well as a listener. People can publish Web pages because it is easy and inexpensive to do so. Free speech advocates do not want the government to make it more expensive or difficult to publish on the Web by requiring age verification schemes or through other restrictions.

According to *Public Agenda Online*, Americans are still making up their minds about what the government should do. The majority say the government should "curtail hate sites" and "protect children from dangerous strangers and pornography." On the other hand, "more than half say that the First Amendment freedoms allowed for books and newspapers should carry over into cyberspace."[1]

Government Studies Search for Answers

In 1998, Congress appointed a nineteen-person group known as the COPA Commission to study technology tools to protect minors online. The members reported their suggestions to Congress in 2000.

According to the commission, technology tools can empower consumers and give them choices.

However, technology alone cannot solve the problem. Government leaders, parents, and industry must work together.[2]

Education is a top priority, said the commission. Law enforcement is also needed. Those who publish obscenity on the Internet should be arrested and prosecuted under existing federal and state laws. New laws might discourage adult Web sites from using aggressive marketing tactics. Two worrisome practices identified in the COPA report are mousetrapping viewers in sexually explicit sites, where closing one window only opens

Society is still trying to figure out how to protect young people from dangerous images and information while maintaining the free speech rights of adults.

another, and using deceptive links to lead users to inappropriate sites.

The commission urged industry members to be responsible. Internet service providers could make filtering and monitoring products easier for parents to find and to use. Adult entertainment publishers could also do more to make sexually explicit material harder for minors to find, either by accident or on purpose.[3]

Education Is the Key

Congress also asked the Computer Science and Telecommunications Board of the National Research Council to research ways to protect children online. A committee was appointed to study the problem. The committee released its findings in 2002. Like the COPA Commission, the NRC found the problem complex.

The committee assigned to study the problem concluded that not one but many solutions would be required. The committee stated:

> Though some might wish otherwise, no single approach—technical, legal, economic, or educational—will be sufficient. Rather . . . an effective framework for protecting our children . . . will require a balanced composite of all these elements.[4]

We need laws, education, and technology to protect young people online, said the report. However, education is the most important of the three. Children and parents need training in media literacy and Internet safety, such as how cult groups recruit members and how predators ensnare their victims. Families, schools, and libraries should adopt guidelines for online behavior.[5] Armed with behavior guidelines, safety education, and media literacy skills, young people are best equipped to avoid unpleasant experiences on the Internet, according to the committee. They wrote:

> An analogy is the relationship between swimming pools and children. Swimming pools can be dangerous for children. To protect them, one can install locks, put up fences, and deploy pool alarms. All of these measures are helpful, but by far the most important thing that one can do for one's children is to teach them to swim.[6]

Although far less important than education, technological tools such as filters have a role to play, said the report.[7] Filters have limitations, but they offer a measure of protection for parents who want to use them, particularly those with younger children.

Public policies or laws can help, too. Enforcing existing obscenity laws will reduce the amount of inappropriate content on the Internet, according to the NRC committee. In turn, minors will be less likely to find it. However, the global nature of the Internet limits what the United States can do alone.

Censorship or Public Safety?

Legal scholar Robert Corn-Revere has observed the tendency of governmental authorities to clash with "technologies of free expression."[8] A century ago, Turkish officials banned typewriters, he notes. Soviet rulers jammed Western radio broadcasts during the Cold War.[9]

The Internet's power to send and receive information makes governments anxious to control speech, says Corn-Revere, "whether that speech takes the form of pro-democracy writings, Nazi memorabilia, or sexually explicit imagery."[10]

In the United States, civil libertarians are wary of attempts to regulate speech on the Internet. Free speech advocates question the value and purpose of laws aimed at "cleaning up" cyberspace in the interest of protecting children. Rather than passing laws, they advocate parental supervision and education to keep minors safe online. The ACLU explains why civil libertarians oppose the censorship of disturbing messages such as violence, sexually explicit material, and art that offends some people's religious beliefs:

> The answer is simple, and timeless: a free society is based on the principle that each and every individual has the right to decide what art or entertainment he or she wants—or does not want—to receive or create.[11]

Another view comes from John Hughes, former editor of *The Christian Science Monitor*. Hughes began to think about "the hidden illness of the new millennium," as he quotes one therapist, after a member of his family linked to a site called "small dogs." It was a porn site. He writes:

> The Internet is awash in sex—more than 400,000 Web sites and counting. Celebrities dabbling in child porn are arrested. Families are destroyed. Therapists' caseloads are

The Bill of Rights—the first ten amendments to the Constitution—assures Americans of the right to freedom of speech. The creation of the Internet has raised a host of new questions about this right.

swamped with cyberporn addicts. And the addiction sometimes goes beyond glassy-eyed computer watching to sexual molestation, bestiality, and even murder. . . The question we should be asking is: Even when it's technically legal, is [pornography] moral and desirable?[12]

Hughes voices a concern shared by many Americans. They see a cause-and-effect relationship between the consumption of pornography—or hate speech or bomb-making instructions—and the output of hardened attitudes, if not antisocial behavior.

On both sides of the debate, people say they value the safety of young people and the principles of the First Amendment. Both want to help children enjoy the benefits of the Internet while avoiding its perils. However, they disagree about what to do.

Where does responsibility lie? What, if anything, should the government do to make it harder for young people to find inappropriate sexually explicit material? What should parents do? Are technology tools such as filters an appropriate solution in schools and libraries? Or should we rely exclusively on Internet safety skills and media literacy to keep minors safe online?

Free speech advocates argue that if adults do not let children make their own decisions, today's young people will not develop the media literacy skills they need to be tomorrow's responsible online citizens. Are they right?

Do we have to have a single solution, or can communities decide for themselves what is best? Will our decisions have an impact on the larger world debate?

What do you think?

A Final Note

The free speech debate affects young people. Attempts to restrict online pornography are done in the interests of protecting children. Mandatory filters on school and library computers limit not only pornographic content but much useful and legal information, too. For instance, filters often block sensitive health information.

However, the government has a legitimate interest in protecting minors. Some young people receive aggressive online solicitations from adults. Children can be targets for cyberpredators and marketers. Some encounter sexually explicit material while doing innocent research. Many people find these materials offensive and in conflict with their moral and social values.

As the National Research Council suggests, we need solutions that allow for diverse standards and opinions. Education, public policy, and technology tools all have a role to play. Above all, responsible thinking and acting is an important first step to help young and old alike reap the rewards of the Internet.

Chapter Notes

Chapter 1. Conflicts in Cyberspace

1. Tracy Cooper, "Tempest in a Web Site," *McKinney Messenger*, March 5, 1998, <http://misd. deltos.com/tempest.htm> (March 6, 2001); and Aaron Smith, telephone interview, February 7, 2002.

2. Smith.

3. Ibid.

4. Home page of C.H.O.W.,<www.geocities. com/lordofthepage> n.d., (February 7, 2001).

5. Ibid.

6. Smith.

7. Ibid.

8. National Research Council, Computer Science and Telecommunications Board, *Youth, Pornography, and the Internet* (Washington, D.C: National Academy Press, 2002), <http://www.nap.edu/openbook/ 0309082749/html/121.html> (December 9, 2002).

9. Ibid.

10. David J. Finkelhor, Kimberly Mitchell, and Janis Worlak, "Online Victimization: A Report to the Nation's Youth," University of New Hampshire, Crimes Against Children Resource Center, June 2000, <http://unh. edu/ccrc/victimization_online_survey.pdf> (February 7, 2003).

11. Bruce Taylor, telephone interview, January 29, 2003.

12. John C. Dvorak, "Sick Porn E-Mails Plague the Net," *PC Magazine*, November 12, 2002, <http://

www.pcmag.com/print_article/0,3048,a=33549,00. asp> (February 2, 2003).

13. Taylor.

14. National Research Council, <http://www. nap.edu/openbook/0309082749/html/72.html>.

15. Ibid.

16. Robert Corn-Revere, "Caught In the Seamless Web: Does the Internet's Global Reach Justify Less Freedom of Speech?" CATO Institute Briefing Papers, No. 71 (July 24, 2002), p. 11.

17. National Research Council, <http://www.nap. edu/openbook/0309082749/html/22.html>.

18. Ibid., <http://www.nap.edu/openbook/0309 082749/html/24.html>.

19. Finkelhor, Mitchell, and Worlak.

20. Judith Krug, telephone interview, February 7, 2003.

21. Leonard R. Sussman, "The Internet in Flux," Freedom House Annual Report, 2001, <www. freedom house.org> (November 10, 2002).

22. Corn-Revere, p. 3.

23. Ibid.

Chapter 2. Exploring the Internet

1. NUA Internet Surveys, "How Many Online?" Scope Communications Group, Dublin, Ireland, 2001, <http://www.nua.ie/surveys/how_many_online/index. html> (January 23, 2003).

2. "Connected to the Future: A Report on Children's Internet Use form the Corporation for Public Broadcasting," p. 2., (Washington DC: Corporation for Public Broadcasting, 2003), <http://www.cpb.org/ed/ resources/connected/> (May 10, 2003).

3. Tim Berners-Lee, *Weaving the Web: The Original Design and Ultimate Destiny of the World Wide Web by*

Its Inventor (San Francisco: HarperSanFrancisco, 1999), p. 4.

4. "Learn the Net: How the Web Works," n.d., <http://www.learnthenet.com/english/web/030www.htm> (February 9, 2003).

5. *Reno* v. *ACLU*, 117 S.Ct. 2329, 853 (1997).

Chapter 3. A New Form of Media

1. *New York Times* v. *United States*, 403 U.S. 713, 716 (1971).

2. Ibid.

3. Ibid.

4. *ACLU* v. *Reno*, 929 F. Supp. 824, 883 (E.D. Pa. 1996).

5. Robert S. Peck, *Libraries, the First Amendment and Cyberspace: What You Need to Know* (Chicago: American Library Association, 2000), p. 142.

Chapter 4. Web Censorship in the United States

1. Robert Hobbes Zakon, *Hobbes' Internet Timeline v6.0*, 1999–2003, <http://www.zakon.org/robert/internet/timeline> (February 13, 2003).

2. National Center for Education Statistics, "Digest of Education Statistics 2001," February 2002, <http://www.publicagenda.org/issues/factfiles_detaill.cfm?issue_type=internet+list=11> (February 13, 2003); Eric C. Newburger, "Computer Use in the United States," *Current Population Reports*, U.S. Census Bureau, October 1997.

3. Marty Rimm, "Marketing Pornography on the Information Superhighway," *Georgetown Law Journal*, June 1995, pp. 1849–1934.

4. HomeNet Press Release, "The HomeNet Project," July 1995, <http://homenet.hcii.cs.cmu.edu/progress/press-release.html> (February 18, 2003);

"The Internet Censorship Saga: 1994–1997," n.d., <www~swiss.ai.mit.edu/6805/articles/cda/saga.html> (March 13, 2001); and David Hudson, "CyberSmut, Protecting Kids, Preserving Freedom—Pornography and the Internet: Tackling an Old Issue in a New Medium," The Freedom Forum Online, June 3, 1998, <http://www.freedomforum.org/speech/series/cda.series.1.asp> (January 10, 2002).

5. Donna L. Hoffman and Thomas P. Novak, "A Detailed Analysis of the Conceptual, Logical, and Methodological Flaws in the Article: Marketing Pornography on the Information Superhighway," July 2, 1995, <http://www.eff.org/Censorship/Rimm_CMU_Time/rimm_hoffman_novak.critique> (February 3, 2003).

6. Ibid.

7. Ibid.

8. Cong. Record, 104th Cong., at S8087-S8092 (Remarks of Sen. Exon) (June 9, 1995).

9. Cong. Record, 104th Cong., at S8330 (Remarks of Senator Exon) (June 14, 1995).

10. Ibid.

11. Ibid.; see also Robert S. Peck, *Libraries, the First Amendment and Cyberspace: What You Need to Know* (Chicago: American Library Association, 2000), p. 126.

12. Communications Decency Act of 1996, Section 223(d), <http://www.law.gwu.edu/facweb/dnunziato/1cda223.htm> (July 8, 2003).

13. Solveig Bernstein, "Beyond the Communications Decency Act: Constitutional Lessons of the Internet," Cato Institute, Cato Policy Analysis No. 262, November 4, 1996, <http://www.cato.org/pubs/pas/pa-262.html> (January 17, 2003).

14. *ACLU v. Reno*, 929 F. Supp. 824, 883 (E.D. Pa. 1996).

15. *Ginsberg* v. *New York*, 390 U.S. 629, 639 (1968).

16. *Reno* v. *ACLU*, 117 S.Ct. 2329, 2343 (1997).

17. Peck, p. 128.

18. *Reno* v. *ACLU*, 117 S.Ct. 2342 (1997).

19. Ibid., 2348

20. Ibid., 2343.

21. Ibid., 2342.

22. Ibid., 2344.

23. *Ashcroft* v. *American Civil Liberties Union*, 535 U.S. 564 (2002).

24. Ibid.

25. Warren Richey, "A Key Case on Kids and Web Porn," *The Christian Science Monitor*, February 28, 2002, pp. 1, 4.

26. Bruce Taylor, telephone interview, February 10, 2003.

27. *Ashcroft* v. *American Civil Liberties Union*.

28. Ibid.

Chapter 5. Libraries and the First Amendment

1. *American Library Association* v. *United States*, 201 F. Supp. 2d 401 (E.D. Pa. 2002), <http://www.paed.uscourts.gov/documents/opinions/02D0415P.htm> (January 30, 2003).

2. Ibid.

3. Lorri Faith Cranor, telephone interview, February 4, 2003.

4. Ibid.

5. Ibid.

6. Ibid.

7. Kelly Isaacs Baker, "Net Nanny Proves It's Mindful When It Comes to Flesh," *Dayton Daily News*, November 22, 2002, p. A1.

8. *American Library Association* v. *United States*.

9. Ibid.

10. Larry Greenmeier, "Filters Fail to Keep Kids Safe," *Information Week*, March 19, 2001, p. 102.

11. *American Library Association* v. *United States.*

12. Ibid.

13. International Communications Research Survey, "Internet: People's Chief Concerns," *Public Agenda Online*, December 1999, <www.publicagenda. org/issues/major_proposals_detail2.cfm?issue_ type=internet&proposal_graphic=mpscreening.gi> (February 13, 2003).

14. *United States* v. *American Library Association*, No. 02-361 (U.S. Supreme Court, June 23, 2003), Syllabus, <http://supct.law.cornell.edu/supct/html/ 02-361.ZS.html> (July 8, 2003).

15. *United States* v. *American Library Association*, No. 02-361 (U.S. Supreme Court, June 23, 2003), Rehnquist opinion, <http://supct.law.cornell.edu/ supct/html/02-361.ZO.html> (July 8, 2003).

16. Ibid.

17. Electronic Frontier Foundation, "Supreme Court Supports Library Internet Blocking Law," Online press release, June 23, 2003, <http://www.eff.org/ Censorship/Censorware/20030623_eff_cipapr.php> (June 24, 2003).

18. American Library Association, "ALA Denounces Supreme Court Ruling on Children's Internet Protection Act," Online press release, June 23, 2003 <http:// www.ala.org/Template.cfm? Section=News&template= /ContentManagement/ContentDisplay.cfm&ContentID =36357> (June 24, 2003).

19. The Library Research Center, "Survey of Internet Access Management in Public Libraries," Report for the American Library Association, June 2000, p. 6.

20. David Biek, "Demographic Characteristics of Internet Users at the Tacoma Public Library, with

Special Reference to the Issue of Internet Pornography," white paper submitted to the National Research Council Committee on Tools and Strategies for Protecting Kids from Pornography and Their Application to Other Inappropriate Material on the Internet, 2001, <http://www7.nationalacademies.org/itas/whitepaper_5.html> (July 8, 2003).

21. National Research Council, Computer Science and Telecommunications Board, *Youth, Pornography, and the Internet* (Washington, D.C.: National Academy Press, 2002), <http://www.nap.edu/openbook/0309 082749/html> (December 9, 2002).

22. Leonard Kniffel, "You Can't Have Sex in the Library," *American Libraries*, March 2001, p. 30.

23. Ibid.

24. Internet Free Expression Alliance, "Kids and the Internet: The Promise and the Perils," Section III, white paper, December 14, 1998.

25. *Mainstream Loudoun* v. *Board of Trustees of the Loudoun County Library*, 2 F. Supp. 2d 783 (E.D. Va. 1988).

26. Ibid.

27. *Board of Education, Island Trees School Union Free School District No. 26* v. *Pico*, 457 U.S. 853 (1982).

28. Ibid., Quoting from *West Virginia Board of Education* v. *Barnette*, 319 U.S. 624, 642.

29. "Library Internet Lawsuit: Judge Brinkema's Decision," Mainstream Loudoun, n.d., <http://www.loudoun.net/mainstream/Library/Internetdecision.htm> (July 8, 2003).

30. *United States* v. *American Library Association*, No. 02-361 (U.S. Supreme Court, June 23, 2003), Souter dissenting, <http://supct.law.cornell.edu/supct/html/02-361.ZD1.html> (July 8, 2003).

31. Ibid.

Chapter 6. Schools, Free Speech, and the Web

1. National Center for Education Statistics, "Digest of Education Statistics 2001," February 2002, <http://www.publicagenda.org/issues/factfiles_detail.dfm?issue_type=internet&list=11> (February 13, 2003); see also National Research Council, Computer Science and Telecommunications Board, *Youth, Pornography, and the Internet* (Washington, D.C.: National Academy Press, 2002), <http://books.nap.edu/books/0309082749/html/19.html> (December 9, 2002).

2. National School Boards Foundation Internet Survey, "Are We There Yet? Research and Guidelines on Schools' Use of the Internet," n.d., p. 2, <http://www.nsbf.org/thereyet/fulltext.htm> (May 14, 2003).

3. Anne Kleiner and Elizabeth Farris, "Internet Access in U.S. Public Schools and Classrooms: 1994-2001," Washington, DC: U.S. Department of Education, National Center for Education Statistics, 2002, p. 9.

4. "ACLU in the Courts: Brandon Beussink.v. Woodland R-IV School District," n.d., p. 2, <http://archive.aclu.org/court/beussinkvwoodland_pi_order.html> (December 16, 2002).

5. Ibid., pp. 1, 5.

6. Ibid., p. 7.

7. Matt Welch, "Off-Campus Speech v. School Safety," *Online Journalism Review*, March 12, 2001, <http://www.mattwelch.com/OJRsave/OJRsave/DahillerSide.htm> (November 21, 2002).

8. Michael D. Simpson, "Cyber Threats On the Rise," *NEA Today Online*, January 2001, <http://www.nea.org/neatoday/0101/rights.html> (December 16, 2002).

9. Ibid.

10. Ibid.

11. Nancy Willard, telephone interview, March 5, 2002.

12. *Beidler* v. *North Thurston School District No. 3*, No. 99-2-00236-6 at 6 (Wash. Super. Ct. for Thurston County, July 18, 2000).

13. Ibid.

14. *Thomas* v. *Board of Education*, 607 F2d 1050 (2 Cir. 1979).

15. Ibid.

16. *Beidler*, No. 99-2-0023606 at 3.

17. *Tinker* v. *Des Moines*, 393 U.S. 503, 506 (1969).

18. Ibid., at 508.

19. Ibid., at 503.

20. *Beidler*, No. 99-2-0023606 at 3.

21. Ibid.

22. *Bethel School District No. 403* v. *Fraser*, 478 U.S. 675, 681 (1986).

23. *Hazelwood School District* v. *Kuhlmeier*, 484 U.S. 260 (1988).

24. *Beidler*, Ibid., at 5.

25. David Hudson, telephone interview, March 1, 2002.

26. David Hudson, "The Effect of Diminishing Student Rights, Fear of the Internet and Columbine," (Freedom Forum, 2000), <http://www.freedomforum.org/packages/first/censorshipinternetspeech/part4.htm, Part IV> (February 7, 2003).

27. Hudson, <http://www.freedomforum.org/packages/first/censorshipinternetspeech/conclusion.htm, Conclusion.>

28. National School Boards Foundation Internet Survey, p. 9.

29. Ibid.

Chapter 7. Online Pornography and Other Controversies

1. American Civil Liberties Union, "Freedom of Expression in the Arts and Entertainment," no. 14, February 27, 2002, <www.aclu.org/news/NewsPrint. cfm?ID=9462&c=42> (February 22, 2003).

2. *Roth* v. *United States*, 354 U.S. 476, 483-485 (1957).

3. *Miller* v. *California*, 413 U.S. 15, 24 (1973).

4. Ibid.

5. Attorney General's Commission on Pornography: Final Report (Washington, D.C.: U.S. Government Printing Office, 1986, vol. 1), p. 229.

6. Nadine Strossen, *Defending Pornography: Free Speech, Sex and the Fight for Women's Rights* (New York: Scribner, 1995), p. 14.

7. American Civil Liberties Union, "Freedom of Expression in the Arts and Entertainment," no. 14, February 27, 2002, <www.aclu.org/news/NewsPrint. cfm?ID=9462&c=42> (February 22, 2003).

8. *United States* v. *Schwimmer*, 279 U.S. 644, 654-55 (1929) (Holmes, J., dissenting).

9. Strossen, pp. 41–42.

10. Barry W. Lynn, "Polluting the Censorship Debate: A Summary and Critique of the Final Report of the Attorney General's Commission on Pornography," *ACLU Public Policy Report*, July 1986, pp. 29–30.

11. George F. Will, "America's Slide into the Sewer," *Pornography: Private Right or Public Menace*, Robert M. Baird and Stuart E. Rosenbaum, eds. (New York: Prometheus Books, 1998), p. 257.

12. Princeton Survey Research/Pew Research Center for the People and the Press, "Internet: People's Chief Concerns," *Public Agenda Online*, October 1999,

<http://www.publicagenda.org/issues/pcc_detail.cfm? issue_type=internet&list=17> (February 13, 2003).

13. Washington Post/Kaiser Family Foundation and Harvard University, "Internet: Major Proposals," August 1998; Princeton Survey Research/Pew Research Center for the People and the Press, "Internet: Major Proposals," *Public Agenda Online*, October 26– December 1, 1998, <http://www.publicagenda.org/ issues/major_proposals_detail.cfm?issue_type=internet &list=4> (February 13, 2003).

14. *Reno* v. *ACLU*, 521 U.S. 844, 117 S.Ct. 2329, 2347 n.44 (1997).

15. "United States Attorneys Obscenity Prosecution Record for Fiscal Years: 1993–2001," Transactional Records Access Clearinghouse, Syracuse University, n.d., <http://www.moralityinmedia.org/index.htm?obscenity Enforcement/usatylis.htm> (January 13, 2002).

16. Aletha C. Huston, Ellen Wartella, and Edward Donnerstein, *Measuring the Effects of Sexual Content in the Media: A Report to the Kaiser Family Foundation, The Henry J. Kaiser Family Foundation*, Menlo Park, California, 1998, p. 40, <http://www. kff.org/content/ archive/1389/content.html> (February 15, 2003).

17. Ibid., p. 6.

18. Ibid., p. 1.

19. Ibid., p. 35.

20. "The Duffel Bag Bombs," Jefferson County, Colorado, Sheriff Web site, n.d., <http://denver. rockymountainnews.com/shooting/report/columbine report/pages/dufflebags.htm> (February 19, 2003).

21. "Narrative Time Line," Jefferson County, Colorado, Sheriff Web site, n.d., <http://denver. rockymountainnews.com/shooting/report/columbine report/pages/narrative_time_line.htm> (February 19, 2003); Dan Luzadder and Kevin Vaughan, "Amassing

the Facts," *Denver Rocky Mountain News*, n.d., <http://denver.rockymountainnews.com/shooting. 1213col1.shtml> (February 19, 2003).

22. Luzadder and Vaughan, p. 5.

23. "Narrative Time Line," pp. 2, 3.

24. Ibid., p. 3.

25. Ibid., p. 12.

26. "Forward," Jefferson County, Colorado, Sheriff Web site, n.d., <http://denver.rockymountainnews. com/shooting/report/columbinereport/pages/forward. htm> (Feburary 19, 2003)

27. Lisa Bowman, "Did the Internet contribute to Littleton?" *ZD Net News*, April 26, 1999, <http:// zdnet.com.com/2100-11-514471.html?legacy= zdnn> (February 19, 2003).

28. Luzadder and Vaughan, p. 5.

29. David Hudson, "Columbine tragedy fuels push for filtering measure in Senate," First Amendment Center, May 28, 1999, <http://www.freedomforum. org/templates/document.asp?documentID=10620> (February 19, 2003).

30. Bowman, p. 1.

31. FBI Web Site, Hate Crime Cases, Los Angeles, California, October 3, 1996, <http://www.fbi.gov/hq/ cid/civilrights/hatecases.htm> (February 20, 2003).

32. "Legal Aspects of Government-Sponsored Prohibitions Against Racist Propaganda on the Internet: The U.S. Perspective," U.S. Department of Justice, February 18, 1998, <www.usdoj.gov/criminal/cyber crime/racismun.htm> (January 3, 2003).

33. Ibid.

Chapter 8. Privacy and Predators

1. "Privacy Online: A Report to Congress," Federal Trade Commission, June 1998, Children's Privacy

Online, "Growth in the Number of Children Online," <http://www.ftc.gov/reports/privacy3/history.htm#Children's Privacy Online> (February 15, 2003).

2. Ibid., <http://www.ftc.gov/reports/privacy3/survey.htm#Children's Survey Findings>.

3. Ibid.

4. Ibid.

5. David Whalen, "The Unoffical Cookie FAQ, Version 2.6," 2002, <http://www.cookiecentral.com/faq> (February 5, 2003).

6. Ibid.

7. *Olmstead* v. *United States*, 277 U.S. 438, 474 (1928).

8. Ibid. at 479.

9. ACLU Online Archives, "Privacy," 1998, <http://archive.aclu.org/issues/privacy/isprivacy.html> (February 15, 2003).

10. CyberTipline, "Success Stories," National Center for Missing and Exploited Children, n.d., <http://www.ncmec.org/html/success_cybertipline.html> (January 13, 2002).

11. J. Robert Flores, telephone interview, January 29, 2003.

12. Deborah Niemann-Boehle, Testimony, Hearing before the Subcommittee on Crime of the Committee on the Judiciary House of Representatives, H.R. 3494 and Related Legislation, April 30, 1998, pp. 22–23.

13. Larry Magid, "Kids' Rules for Online Safety," *SafeKids.com*, 1998, <http://www.safekids.com/kidsrules.htm> (February 19, 2003).

Chapter 9. The Global Debate

1. Digital Freedom Network, "Chinese Webmaster Faints At Trial," Online press release, February 13,

2001, <http://www.dfn.org/focus/china/huangqi-010213.htm> (February 4, 2002).

2. Robert Marquand, "China Tames Wild, Wild Web," *The Christian Science Monitor*, August 2, 2001, p. 10.

3. Robert Corn-Revere, "Caught In the Seamless Web: Does the Internet's Global Reach Justify Less Freedom of Speech?" CATO Institute Briefing Papers, No. 71, July 24, 2002, p. 6.

4. Ibid.

5. Marquand, p. 10.

6. Corn-Revere, p. 6.

7. Human Rights Watch, "Special Issues and Campaigns: Freedom of Expression on the Internet," Online report, 1999, <http://www.hrw.org/world report99/special/internet.html> (November 11, 2001).

8. Corn-Revere, p. 7.

9. Ibid.

10. Ibid.

11. General Assembly of the United Nations. "Universal Declaration of Human Rights," December 10, 1948, <http://www.un.org/Overview/rights.html> (April 25, 2003).

12. Declan McCullagh, "Plague of Freedom," *Internet Underground*, July 31, 1996, <http://www.eff.org/Publications/Declan_McCullagh/www/global/index_old.html> (January 3, 2002).

13. Leonard R. Sussman, "The Internet in Flux," Freedom House Annual Report, 2001, <www.free domhouse.org> (November 10, 2002).

Chapter 10. Conflicting Viewpoints and Common Ground

1. "Red Flags, Policing the Net," *Public Agenda Online*, 2003, <http://www.publicagenda.org/issues/

red_flags.cfm?issue_type=internet> (February 13, 2003).

2. Commission on Child Online Protection (COPA), *Report to Congress*, October 20, 2000, <http://www.copacommission.org/report> (February 7, 2003).

3. Ibid.

4. National Research Council, Computer Science and Telecommunications Board, *Youth, Pornography, and the Internet* (National Academy Press, 2002), <http://www.nap.edu/books/0309082749/html/242.html> (December 9, 2002).

5. Ibid., <http://www.nap.edu/books/0309082749/html/19.html> (December 9, 2002).

6. Ibid.

7. Ibid., <http://www.nap.edu/books/0309082749/html/366.html>.

8. Robert Corn-Revere, "Caught In the Seamless Web: Does the Internet's Global Reach Justify Less Freedom of Speech?" CATO Institute Briefing Papers, No. 71, July 24, 2002, p. 12.

9. Ibid.

10. Ibid.

11. American Civil Liberties Union, "Freedom of Expression in the Arts and Entertainment," No. 14, February 27, 2002, <www.aclu.org/news/NewsPrint.cfm?ID=9462&c=42> (February 22, 2003).

12. John Huges, "Recognizing Pornography When We See It," *The Christian Science Monitor*, January 29, 2003, p. 11.

Glossary

censorship—Preventing another person from reading, speaking, writing, or hearing certain information. Censors range from government officials to parents who forbid particular books or movies.

chatting—A method of communicating where two or more people type messages back and forth to each other. The message from the sender appears almost instantly on the screen of the recipient(s). "Instant messaging" is one type of chatting.

child pornography—Lewd depictions of minors or those that portray minors engaged in sexual activities. Child pornography is illegal.

commercial Web sites—Web sites that earn a profit selling products or services.

cookie—A type of information that lets a Web site "remember" you each time you visit the site. Cookies are sent from a Web server to your browser and are stored on your computer.

cyberporn—Pornographic pictures, stories, e-mail, videos, and animations ranging from indecent to obscene.

cyberstalker—A person who uses the anonymity of the Internet to search out victims that may later be contacted offline.

filtering and blocking software—Programs that provide a buffer between the user and the Internet to control what the user receives.

hacking—A term that has come to mean illegal entry into another computer system.

harmful to minors—Materials that are obscene for minors.

hate speech—Hateful messages directed at certain groups of people because of their race, religion, ethnic background, or for some other reason.

host systems—Computers connected to the Internet, used to store and receive information.

Internet—A global network made up of smaller networks.

network—A group of computers linked by telecommunication lines or other means that can exchange data electronically.

newsgroups—Online discussion groups where people post messages on a topic of interest. Thousands of newsgroups exist on the Internet.

obscenity—Illegal pornographic material that meets the three-part legal definition outlined in *Miller* v. *California*.

Web site—A group of Web pages published by an individual or an organization.

World Wide Web—One of the most popular services on the Internet for finding and retrieving information. The Web is made up of billions of electronic documents stored on many different computers.

Further Reading

Books

Farish, Leah. *Tinker* v. *Des Moines: Student Protest*. Springfield, N.J.: Enslow Publishers, 1997.

Friedman, Samuel Joshua. *Children and the World Wide Web: Tool or Trap?* Lanham, Md., 2000.

Godwin, Mike. *Cyber Rights: Defending Free Speech in the Digital Age*. New York: Crown, 1998.

Graham, Ian. *The Internet: The Impact on Our Lives*. Orlando, Fla., Raintree Steck-Vaughn Publishers, 2001.

Isler, Claudia. *The Right to Free Speech*. New York: Rosen Publishing Group, 2001.

Internet Addresses

American Civil Liberties Union
<http://www.aclu.org>

National Law Center for Children and Families
<http://www.nationallawcenter.org>

National Archives and Records Administration: The Bill of Rights
<http://www.archives.gov/exhibit_hall/charters_of_freedom/bill_of_rights/bill_of_rights.html>

Index